Marcus JWright

REMINISCENCES

OF THE

EARLY SETTLEMENT

AND

EARLY SETTLERS

OF

McNAIRY COUNTY, TENNESSEE.

BY

GEN. MARCUS J. WRIGHT.

"Foot-prints on the sands of time."

Book Publishers

Southern Historical Press, Inc.
Greenville, South Carolina

Please direct all correspondence and book orders to:
SOUTHERN HISTORICAL PRESS, Inc.
PO Box 1267
Greenville, SC   29602-1267

PREFACE.

———

Many years absence from my native county failed to diminish my interest in the old land, and in those I had known in my boyhood. A brief visit there a few years since, revived old memories, awakened interest never lost — but only suspended—and determined me at no distant day to put in print some sketches of the pioneers of McNairy county.

This work would have been impossible, but for the kindly aid which I here acknowledge to have received from Hon. James Warren, Major S. L. Warren, Mrs. Celia Wisdom, Hon. John H. Meeks, Thad. L. Adams, Mrs. Mattie Adams, Miss Flora Shull, Col. Dew M. Wisdom, Mrs. Jennie S. Perkins, and many others. I am specially indebted to Hon. James Warren, who has taken a lively interest in the work and made my duty more that of a compiler than an author.

There are, no doubt, many names not mentioned in this book which deserve a place there. No one will regret this more than myself. I was kindly aided by the newspapers in Purdy and by many friends, in giving notice that I desired information about every one of the old families of the county. If any have failed to send information to me, who could have done so, the fault is not mine, and no one regrets it more than I do.

The little book, such as it is, written *con amore*, is given to its readers with the hope that it may revive and increase the growing interest now manifested for preserving our local history.

Washington City, March, 1882.

Marcus J. Wright

LIST OF ILLUSTRATIONS.

CHAPTER I.

The Act of the General Assembly of Tennessee, providing for the organization of McNairy County, was passed on the 8th day of October, 1823, and is in the following words:

CHAPTER XCVI.

An Act to establish a new County west of Hardin County.

1. Be it enacted by the General Assembly of the State of Tennessee, that a county to be called and known by the name of McNairy, be, and the same is hereby established west of Hardin county; beginning at the southwest corner of Hardin county, running thence north with the west boundary of the same twenty-seven and one half miles; thence west, passing the southeast corner of Madison county, to a point three miles west of the first range line in the ninth district; thence south parallel with said range line to the south boundary of this State; thence east on said boundary to the beginning.

2. Be it enacted, that for the due administration of justice of said county, the Courts of Pleas and Quarter Sessions of said county and the Circuit Courts shall be held at the house of Abel V. Maury, near the centre of said county, until otherwise provided for by law; viz,: The Courts of Pleas and Quarter Sessions on the 2d Mondays in January, April, July, and October, and the succeeding days, and the Circuit Courts on the 3d Mondays in May and November and the succeeding days, in each and every year, under the same rules, regulations and restrictions, and to have and exercise the same powers and jurisdiction that other Courts of judicature of like grades in this State now or hereafter may have.

3. Be it enacted, that the Sheriff of said county shall open and hold an election on the 1st Friday and Saturday in April next, at the place of holding Courts for said county, for the purpose of electing field officers for the militia of said county, under the same rules, regulations and restrictions as are pointed out by law in similar cases; and the militia of said county shall compose the eightieth regiment of Tennessee militia, and be attached to the eleventh brigade.

4. Be it enacted, that it shall be the duty of the commandant of said regiment, having been first commissioned and sworn according to law, to divide his regiment into such number of companies as he shall think best for the convenience of said companies, and it shall further be the duty of said commandant to issue writs of election for company officers according to law, as provided for in other cases of elections for captain and subaltern officers.

5. Be it enacted, that this Act shall take effect and be in force from and after the first day of January next.

JAMES FENTRESS,
Speaker of the House of Representatives.

R. WEAKLEY,
Speaker of the Senate.

The county was named in honor of Judge John McNairy, the eminent Jurist, who was born in Guilford county, North Carolina, in March, 1762. He was appointed by President Washington Judge of the Superior Court of the Western District, and arrived in Nashville in 1788, accompanied by "Mr. Attorney" Andrew Jackson. In February, 1797, he was appointed Judge of the District Court of the United States for Tennessee, which office he held until a few years before his death, which occurred near Nashville November 10th, 1833.

A younger brother, Dr. Boyd McNairy, was born in North Carolina in 1785, and came to Nashville at five years old. He was one of the most famous of the early physicians of the State. A number of his descendants are living: a daughter in New Orleans, Mrs. Goodrich; Major Frank H. McNairy in New Orleans, and Dr. W. S. McNairy in Washington, where he has been for over thirty years in the Navy Department.

The records of the county were destroyed during the late war, and there are no records older than 1858 on file.

The first session of the county Court was held in the early part of the year 1824.

The first settlers were chiefly from North Carolina, South Carolina, Virginia and Middle and East Tennessee. Purdy, the county seat, is located a little east of the centre of the county, on the dividing ridge between the waters of the Tennessee and Hatchie rivers. It was named in honor of Col. John Purdy, one of the early government surveyors. Adamsville is eight miles east of Purdy and four miles from the Tennessee river. It was named in honor of George G. Adams, an old and highly respected citizen. McNairy Station is ten miles northwest of Purdy, on the Mobile and Ohio Railroad. Bethel Springs, a station on the M. and O. Railroad, is four and a half miles west of Purdy. Montezuma is eighteen miles northwest of Purdy, near the Madison county line. Falcon is six miles southwest of Purdy, on the M. and O. Railroad. Ramer's Station is twelve miles south of Purdy, on the M. and O. Railroad. Camden, or Rose creek, is ten miles west of Purdy, on the Bolivar and Purdy road. Chewalla is fifteen miles southwest of Purdy, on the Memphis and Charlestown Railroad. Gravel Hill is fourteen miles south of Purdy, and Stantonville eight miles southeast of Purdy. These constitute the principal towns and villages in the county.

The county comprises about 645 square miles, or 412,800 acres of land. The country immediately around Purdy is hilly and poor. The extreme northern part of the county is level or undulating, and the soil rich and productive. The lands in the southern part of the county are generally level and very productive. The eastern part of the county is hilly, except that portion bordering on Hardin County, which is level and productive. This is the case with the western part of the county also.

The principal streams in the county are Snake creek, which rises some twelve miles southeast of Purdy, and runs northeast and empties into the Tennessee river; Owl creek, which rises about eight miles south of Purdy, and runs southeast and empties into the Tennessee river; Oxford creek, which rises about nine miles south of Purdy, runs southwest and empties into Cypress Creek; Cypress creek, which rises about four miles northwest of Purdy, runs southwest and empties into Hatchie river; Moss' creek, which rises about eight miles southwest of Purdy, runs southwest and empties into Hatchie river; and Hatchie creek, which rises about ten miles northwest of Purdy, and empties into Hatchie river There are many other streams throughout the county, there being no considerable district of country which is not supplied with running water.

The timber is abundant and of good quality, consisting chiefly of oak, hickory, ash, cypress, pine and chestnut.

Cotton, wheat, oats and Indian corn are the principal product of the county.

Apples, peaches, peas, plums, cherries and grapes do well in all parts of the county.

The population in 1870 was white, 11,226; colored, 1,500. Total 12,726.

The Census returns for the fiscal year ending in 1880 are as follows:

Valuation (Assessed)

Real Estate	$1,556,777
Personal Property	$59,243
Total	$1,616,020

Taxation.

Total State and County Tax	$18,292

Debt.

County Debt (floating)	$7,000

Population according to U. S. Census of 1880.

Males	8,605
Females	8,666
Native	17,232
Foreign	39
White	14,845
Colored	2,426
Total Population	17,271

Live Stock.

Horses	2,642
Milch Cows	4,806
Working Oxen	840
Other Cattle	6,925
Mules and Asses	2,308
Sheep	15,300
Swine	25,247

Population by Districts.

1st civil dist	745
2d civil dist	1,375
3d civil dist	772

4th civil dist., including village of Montezuma 942
Montezuma village 148
5th civil dist., including the following villages 2,377
Ramer village 100
Chewalla village 46
6th civil dist., including town of Falcon 1,102
Falcon town 141
7th civil dist., exclusive of villages of Bethel and Purdy................ 1,091
8th civil dist.. 948
9th civil dist 1,346
10th civil dist 1,136
11th civil dist 656
12th civil dist 893
13th civil dist., exclusive of villages of Bethel and Purdy 636
14th civil dist.. 4,325
15th civil dist., including village of Adamsville 996
Adamsville village 174
16th civil dist.. 613
17th civil dist., including village of McNairy 866
McNairy village 145
Bethel village.. 99
Purdy village 243

NOTE.—The villages of Bethel and Purdy were separately returned, but are both in the 7th civil district.

Products.

Tobacco..............................	95 Acres.	34,863 pounds.
Cotton	23,135 ,,	9,419 bales.
Indian corn..........................	33,501 ,,	678,059 bushels..
Oats	5,093 ,,	47,559 ,,
Rye	41 ,,	170 ,,
Wheat	6,726 ,,	30,678 ,,

CHAPTER II.

Names of some of the first Settlers—The Town of Purdy laid off—Col. Purdy's Office—The first Physician, Clerk of County Court, Sheriff, Carpenter, School-teacher and Tradesmen—Building of the Court House, Hotel and County Jail—First Church edifices—Early School-teachers, Physicians..

The first inhabitants in the territory embraced in the county of McNairy settled there in 1820. They were the Kirby's, Beatty's, Gillespie's, McAlpin's, Murray's and Sweat's.

Soon afterwards, many others came in; among them Major Benjamin Wright, John and Samuel Chambers, from Middle Tennessee; James Wisdom from Overton county, Tennessee; Major John Horton, from Giles county; John S. Ingraham; Thomas Anderson, from Bedford county; William Stedman, from Alabama; and Robert and Archibald Houston.

The McKenzie family and Thomas Lane, from Jackson, Tennessee, who opened the first tavern in Purdy, settled in the county about the year 1823 or 1824.

The town of Purdy was laid off by Col. John Purdy and Major Benjamin Wright, and the lots were auctioned off by Wm. S. Wisdom. Col. John Purdy was a citizen of Henderson county, his residence being at a place known as Purdy's Office. On the establishment of a post office at Purdy Major Wright was appointed post master.

Among the earliest residents of Purdy were Dr. Wm. Barnett, who was the first physician who practised in the town, and his brother, Joseph Barnett, who was the first clerk of the county Court. Dr. Barnett came from Williamson county; Joseph Barnett from Wayne. In 1825 Henry Wilson, who was the first sheriff of the county; James Clay the first carpenter in Purdy; J. M. Prince the first school-teacher in the town; the Boyd family, N. E. Griffith, the first merchant, or tradesman of the town, Peter E. Shull, James Reed, Reuben Walker and Henry Kirkland, all settled in Purdy. In the year following 1826, George and John T. Burtwell, from Florence Ala.; Richard S. Harwell, from Springfield Tenn., and Maclin Cross, from Madison county, were added to the citizens of the new town. In 1827 the accessions to population were increased by the settlement in the town of Wm. Ruleman, from Madison county; Jeremiah Cloud, from Alabama; Samuel D. Pace, from Georgia; Laney Moore, from North Carolina; Richard Crump, from Williamson county, Tenn.; also the Denny, Magee and Rains families settled near Purdy. The Wilson and Hill families settled in the county in 1828–29. In 1829 Wiley B. Terry, from East-Tennessee; Jacob Chaney, from Frankfort, Ky.; Doctors Randall and Hedgespeth, from Georgia came in. In 1831 Thomas Combs, Alfred Moore, from Overton county, and John Shull, from Maury county, moved to the county. These were followed, in 1834, by Fountain P. Duke, Robert Turner and Mat. Trice, from Virginia. In 1835 by Capt. Jeremiah G. Adams, from Virginia also.

The first Court held in the county was in 1830, in a rude log cabin. Soon afterwards the court-house (which was burned in 1881) was built by James Reed and Reuben Walker, carpenters, and Henry Kirkland, brickmason. In 1826 Henry Kirkland built the brick hotel on the east side of the square, which was afterwards (during the late war) destroyed by fire, and in 1827 he built the county jail. The first church edifice built in Purdy was a frame building located in the northeast portion of the town. It was a methodist church, and was used also for a school-house. In 1850 the Cumberland Presbyterians erected a house of worship of brick in the centre of the southern part of the town, and the Baptists built a church soon afterwards; but it was so injured during the war that it was never used afterwards as a place of worship.

The early school-teachers of Purdy were Barrett Lock, James Corner, Andrew McKee, David A. Street, R. D. Miller, Isaac Self, Alvy Johnston and Barlow.

The names of the early physicians were Drs. Barnett, Hedgespeth, Randall, Wm. Young, Frank Young, Richard W. Crump, Rufus S. Harwell, Charles C. Crump, R. B. Harris, Wm. McKinney, H. W. Gill, W. C. Kendall, Job Bell, Daniel Barry, and J. F. Duke.

CHAPTER III.

The County occupied by Indians—Western District—County of Hardin—Hardships of Early Settlers—Organization of County—Captains of companies commissioned as Justices of the Peace—The first County Court and first Chairman—The laying off of the Town of Purdy—W. S. Wisdom, Benjamin Wright, John Chambers, Col. John Purdy—First Circuit Court, Judge Joshua Haskell; Maclin Cross, Clerk—Names of early Inhabitants—Emigrants—Stores—Building of Court-House—The first Census and Population—Names of Early Settlers in all parts of the County—Names of all County Officers—Members of the General Assembly—John V. Wright.

NOTE.—I am indebted to Hon. James Warren, one of the old and most highly esteemed citizens of McNairy county, for the following graphic sketch.

The lands now embraced in McNairy county, prior to the year 1819, were occupied by the Chickasaw Indians, it being a part of the territory then known as the Western District. At this date the Indian titles were extinguished and the county of Hardin established, which embraced the territory now covered by McNairy county, and a few daring adventurers began to make their appearance west of the beautiful Tennessee river, for the purpose of making settlements, and with brave hearts and strong arms began to fell the large monarchs of an almost unbroken forest, erect log cabins, and clear small patches of ground for cultivation in corn for bread; but so little was done in this direction the first year that the settlers, few in number and far apart, were compelled to cross the river and go into Middle Tennessee for corn to make the bread. There were but few cattle and hogs, not enough for meat; but the supply was not scant, as game was in abundance, consisting of bear, deer, turkey and smaller game. The names of the first settlers are unknown.

On the 8th day of October, 1823, the General Assembly of the State passed an Act providing for the organization of McNairy county, taking its name from Judge John McNairy, of Nashville. In 1824 the county was organized. Certain men of good character were recommended to the Governor by captains of companies, who were commissioned as Justices of the Peace, who constituted the county Court. (The records of the county Court having been destroyed it is now impossible to get their names.) All the county officers were elected by the county Court. The first Court was held in a log house erected for the purpose on what is now known as the A. V. Murry farm, about four miles south and west of Purdy, the present county site. The first chairman of the county Court was Pressly Christian; Joseph Barrett, clerk, and Henry Wilson, sheriff. The Court was held at this place until about 1825, when the present site was selected and permanently located, and in March, 1825, a sale of town lots was held, Benjamin Wright being the surveyor and Wm. S. Wisdom the auctioneer. On the 4th day of August, 1825, John Yount conveyed to Geo. M. Barnett, A. V. Murry, W. S. Wisdom, Robert Rankin, and Thompson M. Prine, commissioners, 50 acres of land for the location of the county site. John Chambers is said to have originally entered the land on which the town is situated, the fees being paid with money derived from the sale of cheese made by his wife, and hauled to Nashville, a distance of about 150 miles. The town was named in honor of John Purdy, who was a citizen of Henderson county. Another court-house was now built at Purdy of logs, 18 × 20 feet, with clapboard roof and doors and puncheon floor, and although there was but little crime then, a jail was built of about the same material as the court-house.

The first Circuit Court held in the county was presided over by Judge Joshua Haskell; Maclin Cross, clerk. Purdy now began to assume the appearance of a town.

The following named persons constituted the first inhabitants:

Joseph Barnett, Wm. S. Wisdom, T. Prince, John T. Burtwell, George Burtwell, S. D. Pace, William Ruleman. Henry S. Wilson, Steadman, Nat. Griffith, Benjamin Jones, Benjamin Wright and Maclin Cross, who erected log cabins with clapboard roofs and doors, puncheon floors, and stick and dirt chimneys.

The county now began to receive quite a number of immigrants, a large majority of whom were originally from North Carolina.

Hugh Kirby, born December, 1821, and died 4th January, 1870, is said to have been the first white man born in the county.

The first store in the county was owned and operated by John Chambers and Nat. Griffith as partners, their best and principal customers being Indians, who exchanged furs and hides for goods, which were again hauled to Nashville and exchanged for other goods, money being very scarce in the county.

A brick court-house was built in 1830, James Reed being the contractor and Henry Kirkland the builder. The lumber used in its construction was sawed by hand with a whip-saw and bought at from 75 cents to $1.25 per hundred.

The first census was taken in 1830, and showed the population to be 5,316 whites and 381 colored; a total of 5,697.

From the time of my arrival in the county, February, 1827, until 1832, my acquaintance outside of my immediate neighborhood was quite limited, the population increasing rapidly.

The following named persons were among the most prominent citizens in the east part of the county: Beck, Erwin, Gilchrist, Jones, Kerr, Suttrell, McKinzie, Sanders, Veal and Wilson.

Southeast part of the county: Atkins, Burks, Braden, Block, Cunningham, Donald, Dameron, Ealum, Forris, Michie, Sharp, Stubblefield, and Wardlow.

South part of the county: John N. Barnhill, Chambers, Graham, Hooker Hamm, Houston, Huggins, Littlejohn, Prather, Ramers, Springer, Boatman, Darby, Jeans, Forsyth, Henderson, Horn, McCullough, Meeks, Rains, Rotin, and Simpson.

Southwest part of the county: Derryburry, Flowers, Ferguson, Gooch, Kirk, Lock, McGuin, Null, and Young

West part of the county: Bradshaw, Dillon, Hornbuckle, Kernodle, Laughlin, Lockman, McIntire, Moore, Robertson, Saunders, Stovall, Turner, Weatherly, and Wilson.

Northwest part of the county: Clayton, Cobb, Clemons, Floyd, Garner, Hurst, Jackson, Merchuson, Maness, Rowsey, Rankin, Smith, Shoffield, Stewart, Burkhead, Bryant, Cason, Deaton, Estes, Hodges, Johnson, Muse, McIntire, O'Neal, Randolph, Womble, Wade, and Weaver.

North part of the county: Beard, Bullinger, Fowler, Hallis, Ingraham, Jones, Kirby, Lawrence, McHolstead, Plunk, Putman, Patterson, Robinson, Robbins, Sipes, Smith, Sells, Sedford, Walch, and Ward.

Northeast part of the county : Blackshear, Basinger, Combs, Carroll, Cochran, Cox, Hardin, Kemp, Landreth, Merill, Massengill, Phillips, Parish, Riggs, Stanley, Sewell, Scott, Swain, Anderson, Bishop, Clark, Finley, Morrow, Old- ham, Pitts, Smith, Shelton, and Tidwell.

Central or about Purdy: Adams, Barnes, Brooks, Bell, Beaty, Crump, Devault, Denny, Hill, Harwell, Jopling, Kincaid, Murry, McAlpin, Maggil, McAlpin, Sweat, Suratt, Tatum, Walker, Whorton, and Carter.

Sheriffs.

1st.	Henry S. Wilson	from 1824–28
2d.	Laney Moore	„ 1828–32
3d.	Wiley B. Terry	„ 1832–36
4th.	James Boyd	„ 1836–58
5th.	James Warren	„ 1838–44
6th.	N. C. Riggs	„ 1844–50
7th.	Andrew McKee	„ 1850–56
8th.	Wm. D. Jopling	„ 1856–62
	War and no Offices.	
9th.	Samuel Lewis (was killed by a negro riot, and Jas. H. Mitch- ell filled out the time)	„ 1865–68
10th.	James L. W. Boatman	„ 1868–70
11th.	Wm. D. Jopling	„ 1870–76
12th.	J. Randolph Stovall	„ 1876–82

County Court Clerks.

1st.	Joseph Barnett	from 1824–28
2d.	Benjamin Jones	„ 1828–32
3d.	Wm. S. Wisdom	„ 1832–36
4th.	John R. Adams	„ 1836–44
5th.	Aaron A. Saunders	„ 1844–56
6th.	Joseph Walker	„ 1856–64
7th.	R. M. Thompson	„ 1866–70
8th.	Calvin Shull	„ 1870–78
9th.	Job Bell	„ 1878–82

Circuit Court Clerks.

1st.	Maclin Cross	from 1824–36
2d.	Peter E. Shull (elected but died before being qualified, and Larny Moore served out his time by appointment of the County Court)	„ 1836–40
3d.	Lindsey Saunders	„ 1840–48
4th.	A. J. Kincaid	„ 1848–52
5th.	Lindsey Saunders	„ 1852–56
6th.	Milton H. Johnson	„ 1856–64
7th.	D. N. Huddleston	„ 1865–70
8th.	George E. Meeks (who died before his time expired, and G. M. Moore filled his time to the next regular election in 1876)	„ 1870–76

9th.	Wm. D. Jopling	„	1876–78
10th.	Theodore F. Dolby	„	1878–82

Register of Deeds.

1st.	William Murry and A. V. Murry	from	1824–36
2d.	A. W. Murry	„	1836–40
3d.	R. S. Harwell	„	1845–44
4th.	A. M. McKee	„	1844–48
5th	Benjamin Wright	„	1848–60
6th.	Alfred Moore (who died before his term expired, and time filled out by Asa Bell)	„	1860–64
7th.	George M. Moore	„	1866–70
8th.	Edwin R. Turner	„	1870–78
9th.	James H. Curry	„	1873–82

County Surveyors.

1st.	Benjamin Wright.	5th.	Clint. H. Moore.
2d.	Thomas H. Bell.	6th.	Miles Moore.
3d.	John M. Bell.	7th.	F. Hurst.
4th.	Fielding Hurst.	8th.	R. W. Michie.

Record of Surveyors destroyed, so that dates can not be had.

Members of the Lower Branch of Legislature.

1st.	John M. Johnson	from	1835–37
2d.	Wm. H. Beaves	„	1837–39
3d.	John M. Johnson	„	1839–41
4th.	Mathew A. Trice	„	1841–45
5th.	James Warren	„	1845–49
6th.	John H. Meeks	„	1849–53
7th.	Wm. F. Brown	„	1853–55
8th.	John B. Smith	„	1855–57
9th.	John W. Estes	„	1857–59
10th.	J. L. Morphis	„	1859–61
11th.	Wm. D. Jopling	„	1861–63
12th.	Stanford L. Warren	„	1865–67
13th.	Eljah J. Hodges	„	1867–69
14th.	S. L. Warren	„	1869–7)
15th.	Robert S. Houston	„	1870–72
16th.	B. Mauley Tilman	„	1872-74
17th.	Dr. James Mitchell	„	1874–76
18th.	B. M. Tilliman	„	1876–78
19th.	Anson W. Stovall	„	1878–80
20th.	James Warren	„	1880–82

State Senators.

1st.   Orvil L. Meeks, before the war.   3d.   S. L. Warren, since, two terms.
2d.   John Aldredge, since, two terms.   4th.   B. M. Tilliman, present incumbent.

Member of Congress.

John V. Wright, a citizen of this county, served two terms in
  the Federal Congress, and two in the Confederate
  Congress.

County Trustees.

1st.   Robert M. Owens.   5th.   John A. Moore.
2d.   Reuben Hill, John Whorton.   6th.   David Horn.
3d.   David McKinzie.   7th.   J. A. Miller, present incumbent.
4th.   Jacob Lawrence.

Some of these officers have held more than one term.

The first goods ever sold in Purdy were furnished by John Chambers and
sold by Nathaniel Griffith, consisting of but few articles, such as tin cups and
cotton handkerchiefs, &c.

The second stock was furnished by R. I. Chester and sold by W. S. Wisdom.

And then came: John T. Burtwell. H. B. Mitchell. Garret & Kirkland.
Reuben Moore. John Brooks. Moore & Tally. Wisdom & Shull. I. P. Young.
Miller, Moore & Wisdom. Terry & Wisdom. Maclin Cross. Cross & Moore.
Kincaid & Harwell. A. B. McLaughlin. Charley Teas. L. Saunders & Bro. A.
A. Saunders. Hall & Bro. Wisdom & Walsh. Harwell & Shull.

In the county: Little Hatchee. Samuel Lewis. Leon Gay.

North part of county: Josiah Wamble. W. J. Anderson.

At Adamsville: Shelby, Dunn & Rogers. C. H. Dorion. Combs & Stratton

South part of county: Benj. Saunders. Josiah Jeanes. L. Huggins.

At Camden: F. P. Duke.

CHAPTER IV.

Militia organizations and Officers—Names of Lawyers—The Saunders Family—
Three Sketches, by J. S. P.

The first militia regiment organized in the county was No. 107.

1st.	commandant J. T. Burtwell.		Lieutenant-Col. Thomas Hamrick.
2d.	,,	N. C. Riggs.	,,	Thomas Patterson.
3d.	,,	R. D. Wilson.	,,	F. M. Masengale.
4th.	,,	James Johnson.	Not remembered.

Soon after the 108th regiment was organized.

1st.	Colonel Samuel Graham.		Lieutenant-Col. John Derreberry.
2d.	,,	John Campbell.	,,	J. L. Henderson.
3d.	,,	John H. Meeks.	,,	J. N Barnhill.
4th.	,,	O. L. Meeks.	,,	J. D. Young.
5th.	,,	J. M. Kirk.	,,	Isaac Booth.
6th.	,,	W. W. Jeanes.	Not remembered.

The first brigadier-general who reviewed the regiments in this county was—

1st.	Graham, of Perry county.	3d. J. H. Meeks, McNairy.
2d.	R. P. Neely, Bolivar.	4th. W. D. Jopling, McNairy.

The following is a list of the names of Lawyers who practised in the courts of our county in an early date of its history :

Regular—

V. D. Barry, afterwards judge.........	Bolivar,	Tennessee.
Austin Miller...............	,,	,,
David Fentress..........	,,	,,
Henry Barry .... ,;...........	,,	,,

At a later day—

John Fentress.........	,,	,,
Alex. Robertson.........	,,	,,
Joseph 'Cloud.........	Jackson,	,,
Micajah Bullock	Lexington,	,,
William Wiphers.........	,,	,,
James Scott.........	Savannah,	,,
Alex. Harden	,,	,,
A. G. McDougle.........	Waynesborough,	,,
Maclin Cross	Purdy,	,,
B. C. Rives.........	,,	,,

Occasionally in attendance—

W. B. Miller.........	Jackson,	,,
Roger Barton.........	,,	,,
Adam Huntsman.........	,,	,,
S. E. Rose	Lawrenceburg,	,,

Hon. James Warren furnishes the following interesting particulars in regard to the Saunders family, of McNairy county.

My first acquaintance with any of the Saunders family was when I was a small boy in the county of Granger. Stanford L., the eldest son, married the daughter of Henry Lebo, with whom I was living. Soon after Lebo and Saunders moved to Warren county, Middle Tennessee. Some time after Benjamin F. and Hezekiah Saunders also married the daughters of said Lebo. In the year 1827 the three Saunders brothers came to McNairy county and I with them, where I made the acquaintance of the balance of Thomas Saunder's family, consisting of sixteen children (living) as follows:

Sons—

Stanford L..............................	married a	Lebo
Joel K.....................................	,,	Thornhill.
Benjamin F.............................	,,	Lebo.
Hezekiah................................	,,	Lebo.
Lindsey..................................	,,	Landreth.
Thomas..................................	,,	Lebo, a niece of the others.
Aaron A.................................	,,	McKee.
William C., the only one now living.........	,,	Moore.

John, who was killed by the kick of a horse when a boy before they came to this city.

Daughters—

Leah.......................................	married a	Cardwell.
Ellen......................................	,,	Ingraham.
Elizabeth................................	,,	Ramsey.
Nancy....................................	,,	Anderson.
Sarah.....................................	,,	Cardwell, nephew of the above.
Katharine...............................	,,	McCraw.
Polly	,,	Maness.
Rachel...................................	,,	Tennyson.

The family in general was above average in point of intellectual ability, industry and business, though none of them had more than a neighborhood school education.

In religious opinion they were Baptists, and all of the sixteen brothers and sisters were baptized into the church, except Joel K., who was a believer in Christ but never joined the church.

In politics they were divided, and they were a class of men who held on to well-established convictions with great tenacity.

At one time they were the most numerous family ever in the county.

John Saunders, an older brother of Thomas, had but a small family, and I never knew of but two of them marrying: Benjamin married a Miss Landreth; Hannah married C. H. Dorion.

Wm. C. Saunders, of McNairy county, furnishes the following memoranda of the history of his family:

Thomas Saunders, who emigrated to McNairy county, Tennessee, was of a very ancient family in England, having descended from Laurence Saunders, who suffered martyrdom in Queen Mary's reign for preaching the gospel. Thomas' great, great-grandparents were Huguenots, emigrated from England in 1659 to South Carolina and settled about where Charleston now stands. They died in Savannah, Georgia, before the revolutionary war. He married Elizabeth Rook in his 18th year; she was in her 16th year. She was also of English descent; her mother was a Stanford, related to Lord Stanford of London. She was born in Maryland. Their offspring were 17 children—9 sons and 8 daughters—16 raised families. They emigrated from Chatham county, N. C., in 1816 to Granger county, East Tennessee; settled on Clinch River; emigrated to West Tennessee in 1826.

A PIONEER FAMILY.
BY MRS. JENNIE S. PERKINS.

Near the close of the eighteenth century, Thomas Saunders and Elizabeth Rook were married and settled in Chatham county, North Carolina.

The young husband was the son of Benjamin Saunders, a staunch Quaker; the wife was a lineal descendant, on the father's side, of Admiral Rook, of the English navy; on her mother's side, of a younger brother of Lord Stanford and Marie Wills, of Germany.

Thomas had violated the rules of his society by uniting himself with one of a different faith, and was promptly excluded and denied its temporal benefits as well.

Elizabeth was an orphan whose only dower was industry, intellect and great personal beauty.

With only youthful strength and energy to rely upon they began the arduous task of rearing a family on the worn-out soil of their native State.

Their children increasing faster than their means, they removed to Tennessee, whose natural advantages gave superior promise to the unrequited toilers' in the older States.

They stopped a while amid the wild mountain scenery and rich valleys of the eastern division, but the climate being rigorous they sought further, and finally decided upon McNairy county as their permanent home. This was about the year 1825.

Their family had increased to seventeen children, sixteen of whom were living; sons and daughters were married, and with their growing families were settled near them. Here a most encouraging prospect opened before them.

A virgin soil of great fertility, landscapes of marvelous beauty made up of green savannas and towering forests of the finest timber, in whose coverts game was swarming, affording the hunter delightful pastime; while the streams teemed with fish tempting the angler to while away a pleasant hour on the green mossy banks beneath the spreading beeches that hung over the bright water.

The hardy sons of the toil-worn father began to look about them, and build up homes and reputations for themselves.

Although their early opportunities had been very meagre, the " *Old Field School* " of former times being the only institution of learning ever open to them, they had most assiduously tried to educate themselves; their excellent mother sparing no pains to impress upon their minds the necessity of self-culture. They succeeded so well in overcoming their early defects, that they were called to fil many positions of honor and trust, which they did in a creditable manner. Mean-- while their families increased while health and competence smiled on the pleasant homes they had reared in this land of promise.

The gifted mother had passed away; but the aged father sat in the midst of his numerous descendants, like a patriarch of old.

A few years before his death, which occurred in 1848, his children, grand-children, and great-grandchildren numbered one hundred and twenty.

As a family their traits were strongly marked, being ambitious, proud spirited, energetic, deeply devotional and strongly attached to each other and home.

Their personal likeness was very striking, so much so that the most unobserving stranger rarely failed to perceive it.

In religious faith the whole family were Baptists, and all were believers. In politics the father and six of his sons were Democrats, the other two sons were Whigs.

During the war the surviving brothers were divided, three espousing the cause of the South, and three remaining loyal to the United States Government.

They were unyielding in their principles, and vehement in their advocacy, and were ready to make great personal sacrifice for their belief.

Few families have added so much to the population of the section of their choice, or have sent out so many representatives to other states; and fewer still retain through so many generations the mental and physical characteristics of their forefathers, as the descendants of these pioneers of McNairy county.

LINDSEY SAUNDERS.

Lindsey Saunders, who was born in North Carolina in the year 1806, and removed from thence to Tennessee in early boyhood, was endowed by nature of sound jugdment and an indomitable will.

He had a feeble frame, but began holding office as soon as eligible, and was in various positions of official trust until increasing infirmities compelled him to retire.

He had in the meantime attended closely to his landed interests, and occasionnally engaged in selling goods.

Having by the sheer force of will and untiring energy wrested fortune from an adverse fate he had little charity for the failures of others.

He possessed great sincerity of character, and a stern, unyielding temper, was a devoted friend, and decided enemy, inclined to befriend the weak and oppose the strong, and like his Quaker ancestry, opposed to slavery.

Before the war he was an " *old line Whig*," and during the same a staunch adherent of the Union, and was ready to make any sacrifice for the principles he conscientiously believed to be right.

He was neat and methodical in all he did, and very careful of his dress. In person, tall and commanding, very dignified in manner and conversation, of august presence, the face and expression indicating the man. He was strictly temperate; and by exercising great care prolonged his life to his 59th year, then passed quietly away, leaving an example of truth and integrity worthy to be emulated by the rising generation.

Lindsey Saunders.

AARON A. SAUNDERS.

Aaron Saunders, who was born many years later, was also of a delicate frame, but had excellent business capacity.

Being associated with the elder brother in official and mercantile pursuits, and having the same political belief, they were very closely united for a long period and although there existed such a disparity of years, mental characteristics, and general deportment, the two brothers were often mistaken one for the other.

Aaron for many years filled the office of county clerk in the most acceptable manner, and was also largely engaged in merchandising; and was in all respects in the prime of life a most successful man.

He was a very popular minister of the gospel, and by his winning address made hosts of friends.

He was flexile in temperament, inclining to go with the popular tide instead of opposing it; a Free Mason, and pro-slavery in principle, and during the war espoused the cause of the South.

He was tall and elegant in person, very handsome, prepossessing, courtly and polished in manner, retaining in spite of physical decline to the close of life the tenderness that made him beloved by a wide circle of friends and relatives who will not look on his like again.

CHAPTER V.

HON. JAMES WARREN.

The following sketch of Hon. James Warren was published in the *Falcon World*, September, 1880.

Col. James Warren was born in Claiborne county, East Tenn., June 12th, 1810. His father emigrated to that section at an early day, and died when the subject of this sketch was three years old, leaving a wife and eight children. At the age of seven Col. Warren was taken by the County Court and bound to Henry Lebo, a farmer of that county. He moved to Granger county, and thence to Warren county, Middle Tenn., and located at the foot of Cumberland Mountains. Soon after his wife died, and his daughters married, thus leaving him without a house-keeper. He then rebound Col. Warren to David Woadly, with whom he remained two years. His treatment was so cruel that he left Woadley and returned to Lebo and asked him to do something better for him, which he did by binding him to his son-in-law, S. L. Sanders, who was a good man. With him he came to McNairy county in 1827, and served him faithfully until he was twenty one years old.

Soon after arriving at manhood he was elected by the County Court to the office of constable, which he held for two years. In 1836 he was appointed deputy Sheriff, and in 1838 was elected to the office of Sheriff, and by re-election held the office six years. A part of the duties of the office at that time was to collect the State and county taxes, every dollar of which found its way to its proper place.

In 1845 he was elected to the Legislature, and again in 1847. He introduced several bills during each session, which met but little opposition. He was the author of the measure which secured to the occupant holders a title to their for the fees of the office. That act alone saved to the people of McNairy $50.000, and to every other county south and west of the Congressional Reservation line that amount or more.

Up to 1860 he was identified with the Whig party and opposed to secession. During the war he used his influence to protect citizens from arrest and other wrongs. He made several trips to Memphis and elsewhere for the release of prisoners unjustly held by the Federal forces.

He is eminently a man of principle, and acts from a profound sense of duty.

R. D. MILLER

writes the following interesting letter:

WEST HARTFORD, VT., *July* 30, 1881.

General M. J. WRIGHT,

DEAR SIR: I commence writing in response to your kind request, that I would give you, for use in your proposed "Reminiscences of McNairy county, Tenn.," a sketch of *my own* recollections of it.

My college course, in Amherst college, Mass., was completed in August, 1848, and "the world was all before me, where to choose my place of rest, and Providence my guide." An elder brother of mine had been living in Tennessee and his P. O. address, the last time he sent us a letter, some years previous, was *Hamburg, McNairy county*. In September, that year, I started in search of him with the hope of *finding* him, and also some remunerative employment for myself. I need not relate the incidents of my romantic journeying and voyaging by stage, steamer, and railroad, till I reached the county named.

My stage ride from Memphis, mostly by night, was a *hard* one; and the driver left me, one night about one o'clock, at what he thought would be the most convenient point from which to reach Hamburg, a place away from the stage route.

Weary, hungry, and with but twenty-five cents left, I rapped at the door of a man, whose name was Phelps, and met with a cordial reception from him, his place being somewhere between Bolivar and Camden, I think. When I informed him that I was from Vermont, he said he was from Massachussets and that, whenever he met a man from that State, he welcomed him as a *brother*, and any one from any other New England State as a *half*-brother. He went to Tennessee as a clock peddler, found his wife there, and was raising up an interesting family of children. As I informed him of the object of my mission there, as that of first finding my brother, James M. Miller, he said he had seen "*Jeems*" Miller, and thought he was then teaching school not many miles off. His social friendliness cheered my drooping spirits greatly, and I got some good sleep the last part of the night. The next morning, after breakfast, he brought up two horses, which he and I mounted and rode away into places where I should have been utterly *lost, alone;* but, in an hour or two, by inquiry at a log house to which we went,—a strange sight to me then—we learned that my *lost brother* was residing in that part of McNairy county, and teaching school there.

Mr. Phelps continued with me till we found the way *improved*, and he could direct me plainly, and then returned homeward with the horses, while I walked on, till 1 reached my brothers home, also a log house, apparently in the midst of an almost boundless forest !

Mr. Phelp's had a Southerner's generosity; and showed it in refusing to take anything for his service in my behalf; and so my twenty-five cents remained intact for future use ! I reckon, or *guess*, (as a Yankee would say) that he may have carried something of that generous spirit even from the old Bay State. He must have been a good neighbor and useful citizen, and I should suppose that his *sons*, if living, would be found the same. I would like to meet him to day and thank him for his brotherly kindness to me, when I was so nearly destitute, not *knowing* that I had any acquaintance within 1,500 miles, thirty-three years ago !

My brother, a feeble man bodily, intelligent, industrious, honest, patriotic, a planter and school-teacher, a good number of years in that county, but now residing in Hardiman, doubtless has left the savor of a good name among his old neighbors there. In his quiet, unemotional way, he was always ready for every good word and work ! Some of his children are natives of McNairy.

I found him not rich, and, of course, I soon began to feel that I must be looking for something to do. His impression was that the Purdy Academy was in want of a Principal. In a few weeks I was employed in so responsible a position concerning which my first conference was with Hon. James Warren, the chairman

James Warren

of the Trustees and Representative in the State Legislature. My stipulated reward for service then was $30 a month, and boarding myself out of it—*small*, but much better than nothing. The second session my pay was increased to $40 a month ; and out of what I received after meeting the expense of board and all other outgoes, I did something towards paying debts incurred during my college course of study.

I am glad to learn from my nephew that Mr. Warren's sound sense and practical talent are still appreciated by the people and called into use. I remember his countenance so expressive of unassuming modesty and downright honesty, making him always trustworthy. May his sons, if war and disease have spared them—whom I had a *little* share in training— more than fill his place.

Wm. S. Wisdom seemed to be the leading *financier* of the county, having a lien on many plantations and furnishing many of the settlers money and merchandise, by means of which they were tided over their pecuniary and sumptuary difficulties for a while. He had a business talent which, in other circumstances, might have made him a millionaire. A quiet, prompt, straight forwardness characterised his business affairs. My judgment as to his sons, Dew and Peter, from my knowledge of them as my pupils, would be that they came to develop a business talent and taste unlike those of the father, supposing them to have become men of business. One of them might have enjoyed spending money better than earning it. I should like to know how the boys there, to whom I became much attached as a teacher, came out temporally and spiritually. How the Pace boy came out, of whom one of his playmates complained to me that he had been throwing *rocks* at him ? How the Adams boy came out, whom I exhorted to break off the filthy habit of chewing tobacco, as I saw it running down the corners of his mouth, and from whom I then received the reply that he had *tried* and found that he *couldn't !* How the Connor boys came out, who were just as honest, peaceable and faithful as their father was in *his* sphere. How Baker, the eldest member of the school, walking a long distance from home, daily, slow but sure, and anxious to become a *surveyor*, came out.

I am glad to learn that one at least of my Purdy boys has reached an honored place as a soldier : "Marcus !" and yet I am inclined to think that he was scarcely his *father's* equal, in natural, soldierly qualities. The old man, as I recall his person, seemed made to be "*every inch*" a soldier—one of nature's nobleman.

What a quiet, unpretending tradesman Maclin Cross was—not then Judge. When, at the commencement of Taylor's administration, he was purposing to seek the office of postmaster, I remember his questioning me about the Postmaster-General, under Taylor, Jacob Collamer, a *Vermont* man, such a man as *any* State might well be proud of. It may be that, as a Vermonter myself, I wrote him *a line* in Mr. Cross's behalf. That he obtained the office I am quite sure. The clearness and candor of his mind, with other things desirable, would have been helpful in making him a good *judicial* officer. His son was a good scholar, in all respects, promising to make a man of more impressive personal presence than the father. Mr. Riggs, a thick set, short man and a good, zealous methodist— if I mistake not—how pleasantly and happily he seemed to do the duties and meet the perplexities of life, and he had a boy, who was capable of being as cheerfully useful as his father was.

There was Elder Saunders, Baptist preacher and county clerk, almost every day—Sabbath excepted—in his office north of the Court House. Everybody had confidence in him as a man of christian integrity ; though some may have feared an early failure of his lung power, from its being excessively *overtasked*, in parts of his earnest preaching exercises. I am reminded of a saying ascribed to Dr Lyman Beecher, that some preachers seem to forget that it is the lightning, not the thunder, that strikes. Brother Sanders is unusually fortunate if he is still *blowing* the gospel trumpet, so that the " dead in trespasses and sins," shall hear and live. He disliked slavery and hoped for its disappearance, like many of his neighbors ; but, as the circumstances were, he felt that he might as well *pay for* his colored help as to *hire* it. He said to me that he purposed to treat his two servants as fellow-servants of Christ, and yet was not fully *satisfied* with his position in that respect. As a northern man, I did not see how I could then help him to better his condition. If he is living, he is pleased, perhaps, as I am, that so unnatural and troublesome a thing *has* disappeared, though so differently from what we hoped for— from the way which *wisest* men would have chosen.

Father Kerr, the old School Presbyterian preacher, and a farmer, preached to us occasionally, and we always knew that he meant to give us solid, nourishing strengthening truth. He was not an awakening speaker, but one under whose preaching the weary might feel inclined to fall asleep. Some of us once attended a lively protracted meeting under his superintendence, out at his chief preaching station, near the place of his residence. Dr. Gray, of Memphis, a man of pulpit *power* was one of the speakers on that occasion.

Brother Johnson, the Methodist Circuit Rider, was a good young man, alway doing his best, but inclined to bridge over the gaps in connected thought, with saying : *"And so forth and so on."*

We were favored, in those days, with quite a *variety* of preaching, all in the old Academy building, and there was always something *good* in it, for the *help* of those who would *receive* it.

The way by which each man's herd of wandering swains was kept from being lost, interested me when I went to Tennessee. Early in the morning I would hear a cry, which would have startled me if it had resembled the cry of " fire ",that I had heard ; but it was not such a cry. I imagine that it was more like the Indian *whoop*. It was the varying cry as each man's voice varied, of several men in the village, designed to bring each one's herd *home;* and it was not in vain. By inquiry I soon ascertained the object of it, and became much interested in observing how each herd separated itself from all others, and gathered "to its own place," led by the voice of its owner, distinguished by it as *differing* from al others. Happy would it be for multitudes of the human family, if they were a wise, practically, in discovering the voice that calls each wandering one back to the place of abundant supplies—the home of duty, safety and abiding peace.

The last man I saw in Tennessee was Dr. R.W. Crump. By the generous aid of my brotherly, fatherly landlord Kincaid, I was conveyed on horseback through deep mud from Purdy to the Tennessee river in February, 1850, expecting my baggage to follow me soon. Being disappointed as to the arrival of my trunk in time for the first steamer passing Crump's Landing down the river I was oblige to tarry several days with the Doctor. My bill there was *small, indeed,* and the time passed pleasantly. Had I known what was *to come* I might, perhaps, have gone up, a short distance, to Pittsburg Landing, and looked over the field of fire and carnage that has now made that part of McNairy county memorable. It is well that we *know not* what is coming. In conversation with Dr. Crump on religious themes, it came to appear to us that while I was a Congregationalist— very much the same as Presbyterian—he was a Methodist. He expressed no dissatisfaction with his ecclesiastical relation ; but said he regarded the educational principles and methods of the Presbyterians as much superior to those of the Methodists, and that he would like to have his children trained according to the former. I may have heard a Methodist *preacher*, in Tennessee, speak depreciatingly of an educated Gospel Ministry ; but it is pleasent to know that the great Methodist denomination has been coming more and more to advocate and work for *a thorough intellectual training* for the preacher as well as the lawyer and the medical practitioner.

My late, short acquaintance with Dr. Crump and his family was a most agreeable closing up of the last chapter of my experience in McNairy county before committing myself on ship-board to the then greatly swollen waters (58 feet above low water mark) of the Tennessee river, bearing me back towards the home of my childhood, where the snow drifts of winter and the green hills and mountains of summer are marked, and to me attractive characteristics !

These reminiscences may not interest others as they do me, being so far away in the past and so imperfectly sketched. With a better memory and plenty of time something *better* might have been done. What I have written is written, and is at the service of one who, I am sure, will use it wisely.

Very truly yours,

R. D. MILLER.

P. S.—I was occasionally in S. D. Pace's tailoring shop, and remember him a a very *social* man and a very strong Freemason. He once said to me, in substance, that he wanted no better *religious* faith and practice than to be a good Freemason, and his personal acquaintance with that order *should* have made him a more correct judge of its excellencies than one outside like me. I was in the family one evening, when *John*, then clerk in Wisdom's store, boarding at home, going out after supper, put a large sweet potato in his pocket to roast in the stove for lunch *later* in the evening. He was a young man, who did not seem likely to *worry* himself into the grave— a good eater, probably, and therefore strong for work.

Calvin Shull—whose father went to West Tennessee in search of health, and died there some years before—I recall as a gentlemanly, candid young business man, likely to take a leading place, if bodily health might be his, among his fellows. I recollect his speaking to me sometimes of the fact that a Louisville phrenologist, who was lecturing in Purdy, had given the signal of his being a member of the order of the Sons of Temperance, contrary to the *rules* of the order as an evidence of dishonesty. I presume Calvin's widowed mother always felt that she could safely rely upon her son's integrity.

You are aware that I was generally *about my own business* in Purdy ; and I therefore failed to become much acquainted with more than a few of the people, which fact makes me *defitient* on *reminiscences*. I have sketched the inclosed *hastily*, and commit it to your hands for *correction, contraction, emendation,* &c.

Wishing you the best success in this and all other good works.

Very truly, yours, again,

R D. MILLER.

The following letter was also writ'en by Rev. R. D. Miller, of West Hartford, Vermont.

After an absence of more than thirty years, my recollections of Purdy and its people are many of them clear, and nearly all pleasant. Mr. Warren, then representative in the State Legislature, was the first man with whom I counselled as to my *teaching* in the male department of the Academy. His boys were among my pupils. The brick hotel, on the corner west of the court-house, was my well-conducted boarding place. Jack Kincaid cannot have been forgotten by a *great many* in West Tennessee, as one of the most kind-hearted, enterprising, public-spirited men of McNairy county. His bartender, (without anything intoxicating) Col. Swan, how quickly, with his sharp eye, smiling face and gentle voice, he made all new comers feel at home! Uncle Jimmie Reed—what a sunbeam he was by his genial sociability and practical wisdom, in that house! He was a Northern man originally, and a *national* man politically, when he made his home further South; though a strong Whig and an ardent admirer of Tom Corvin, of Ohio, his native State.

I would like to know all about the Wisdoms, the Crosses, the Paces, the Connors, &c. Mr. Connor was precentor at all meetings, reading two lines of a hymn at a time, and then "leading off." The only familiar name of anyone, now a resident of Purdy, that I notice in your paper, is that of lawyer McKinney. He was a young man when I was there, (if he is the one I knew) promising to become, with good habits and hard work, a *prominent* man in his profession. His brother—the Doctor—a man, as I recall him, steady, quiet, reliable, ever aiming to do the best possible for his patrons, is, perhaps, still practising the healing art with increasing success. I would be glad, at least, to be assured of this.

Had I been made with my nephew's poetic talent, I might, perhaps, give you an interesting sketch of my experience and observations since I was graduated at Amherst College, Mass., in the summer of 1848, and turned my way that fall towards your State in search of a brother still living there; but, as it is, I forbear.

Respectfully,

R. D. MILLER.

W. HARTFORD, VT., *March 1st*, 1881.

WM. T. ANDERSON.

Wm. Taylor Anderson, one of the early settlers of McNairy county, Tenn., was born in Sullivan county, T. nn., May 24th, 1804. While a boy his father, Thomas Anderson, moved to Bedford county, Tenn., and settled on Duck River, near Wartrace.

He had a large family and was very poor. At the age of 18 years, Wm. Taylor Anderson left his father's roof and crossed the Cumberland Mountains on foot in search of a new home in the rich and wild valley of the Mississippi. This he found at his uncle's, Samuel Anderson, who had settled near old Mount Pinson, in Madison county. Here he lived for nearly twelve months, working hard in clearing up the forest at the rate of $50 per year. In the later part of the year 1822 he moved up in McNairy county, and worked with Jas. Wisdom, who had made a settlement on Tar Creek, 11 miles north of where Purdy is now situated. While living here he married Miss Mahala Wisdom and formed a partnership with her brother, Wm. S. Wisdom, in the distillery business on a small scale, as neither of them had any capital except their energy and labor; out of this they made some money.   A short time after his marriage with Miss Wisdom they moved one mile nearer Purdy, on the Purdy and Miflin road, to the now old homestead of Wm. T. Anderson, and lived here in a tent until he was able to erect a small cabin or hut.   Here he began opening a farm and building, and accumulated enough to be able to go back for his aged father and mother whom he had left behind in Bedford county, and moved them to his humble home in West Tenn.   He was an uneducated man, having attended school only six weeks in his life, but by studying at night after his hard day's work was over, soon learned to cipher, read, and write, and afterwards made a useful constable in that district, and was for years a valuable member of the County Court of McNairy county after the county was organized.

By hard work and rigid economy he accumulated a considerable estate, being worth at the beginning of the war forty or fifty thousamd dollars, consisting of a fine dwelling house, lands, negroes, stocks, etc.   He was a good farmer and always had plenty of everything around.   For a number of years in the early settlement of McNairy, he ran successfully a small store on his farm, and his place became a postoffice and voting precinct of the 8th Civil District, known as Anderson's store.

In politics, he took an active part, being an old line Whig, and a great friend of internal improvements in Tennessee.   He was a strong advocate of education, having sorely felt the need of it during all of his life.

Being almost broken up by the war, he moved to Jackson, Tenn., in 1869, where he died of pneumonia April 8th, 1870, aged 66 years.

His widow, one of the most faithful and industrious of women, still lives in Jackson, Tenn., at the advanced age of 76 years, being the only surviving member of her father's family .

Of the six sons of Wm. F. Anderson four are now living. Jas. W., the oldest, for a number of years a successful merchant and banker and a valuable citizen of Madison county, died June 16th, 1879.   Geo. S., killed at the battle of Murfreesboro, while fighting for the Confederacy.   Thos. B. and Neil P. are useful business men and citizens in Fort Worth, Texas. John, a farmer, lives at Henderson, Tenn.   Hugh C., the youngest son is a practicing attorney-at-law in Jackson, and was a member of the 41st and 42d General Assemblies of Tennessee, from Madison county.

The five daughters married, raised large families, and became useful members of the Church and society.

CHAPTER VI.

The Sixth Tennessee (Federal) Cavalry—Confederate Troops—Sketches of the families of McCann, Judge James F. McKinney, Rev. Francis Beard, Alex. McCuller, Sr., Lewis B. Carter, John and Jonathan Walsh, Robert G. Simonton, Duke, Price, Turner.

Major Stanford L. Warren furnishes the following interesting particulars in regard to the 6th Tennessee (Federal) Cavalry:

After the battle of Shiloh and the retreat of the Confederate Army south, Fielding Hurst, of McNairy county, was commissioned by Andrew Johnson, Governor of Tennessee, to recruit and organize this regiment. By the 1st of October, 1862, he had succeed in recruiting and organizing companies A, B, C, D and G.

W. K. M. Breckenridge, of Perry county, had also been recruiting for a regiment on the east side of the Tennessee river, in the counties of Hardin, Wayne and Perry, and had organized companies E, F and H.

Thomas H. Boswell, of Weakly county, had also been recruiting, and organized companies F, K, L, M.

These companies being consolidated, completed the organization of the 6th Tennessee cavalry, with the following named officers:

Fielding Hurst.......................................Colonel.
W. K. M. Breckenridge..........................Lieutenant-Colonel.
Eldridge S. Tidwell...............................Major.
R. M. Thompson................................... ,,
Thomas Williams...................................Surgeon.
Joseph E. Morvin..................................Assistant-Surgeon.
W. J Smith..Reg. Q.-Master.
Thomas M. Clayton................................Reg Com.
James J. Smith.....................................Chaplain.
S. L. Warren..Adj.
Ben. S. Walker.....................................Sergeant Major.
John F. Tidwell....................................Hosp. Stewart.
John R. Ray...R. Q..M. Sergeant.
John A. Lokey......................................R. Com. Sergt.

This organisation was changed materially during the war by death, resignation and otherwise, so that at the close of the war the organization was as follows:

W. J. Smith.... ....Colonel.
O. H. Scheorer.....................................Lieutenant-Colonel.
Mack. J. Liening...................................Major.
Stanford L. Warren................................ ,,
L. O. Summers.....................................Assistant-Surgeon.
John H. Thorington...............................Adjudant.
Richard W. Eskredge.............................R. C. Sergeant.
William A. Newson...............................Reg. Quart. Master.

Company A.

Had during the war the following officers:

A. M. Thompson..Captain.
B. J. Riggs... „
Samuel Lewis... „
James J. Smith...1st Lieutenant.
C. H. Deford...1st „
Thomas Craugh..2d „
Wm. H. Swaim...2d „

Company B.

Harry Hodges...Captain.
Elijah J. Hodges.. „
Francis M. Tucker..1st Lieutenant.
Samuel D. Hanna..2d „
Wm. W. Kirby...2d „
John Hudelleston...2d „

Company C.

Nathan M. D. Kemp...Captain.
Wm. T. Smith...1st Lieutenant.
Thomas Craugle...1st „
James M. Sandes..2d „

Company D.

Leoi Hurst...Captain.
James L. W. Boatman.. „
Zachariah Norcott..1st Lieutenant.
James R. Norcott...1st „
John P. Gibbs..1st „
James L. Hardwich..2d „

Company E.

John D. Poston...Captain.
Francis A. Smith... „
William Cleary...2d Lieutenant.

Company F.

David J. Dickenson...Captain.
Edward L. Hardin...1st Lieutenant.
R. O. F. Roswell...1st „
John W. Youngblood...2d „

Company G.

Elijah Roberts...Captain.
Wm. Chandler... „
Wm. C. Webb.. „

J. L. W. Boatman...1st Lieutenant.
Wm. F. Balright..2d   "
Isaac J. Shull...2d   "

Company H.

Joseph G. Berry. ....Captain.
Risden D. Deford..   "
Calvin Hanna..1st Lieutenant.
Nicholas Pitts...2d   "
Wm. A. Newsour...2d   "

Company I.

Orlando H. Scherer...Captain.
Stanford L. Warren..   "
William J. Campbell..1st Lieutenant.
Miles Wood..2d   "

Company K.

Thomas H. Boswell ....Captain.
Albert Cook...   "
John W. Barham...1st Lieutenant.
James E. McNair..2d   "

Company L.

John W. Moore..Captain.
John H. Edwards...   "
Thomas B. Waggoner..1st Lieutenant
George T. Wan..1st   "
James N. Julin..2d   "

Company M.

William C. Holt...Captain.
Thad. C. McMahon..   "
Hugh. L. Neely...1st Lieutenant.
James A. Mangun...2d   "

CONFEDERATE TROOPS.

Every effort has been made to obtain lists of Confederate organizations from this county, but without success.

It is thought that the various companies and battalions organized in this county for Confederate service would reach something like two regiments.

Alphonso Cross and Dew M. Wisdom each raised and commanded companies of infantry; the former in the 154th Tennessee regiment, the latter in the 13th Tennessee.

Col. A. N. Wilson commanded a battalion of cavalry from McNairy.

The McCANN FAMILY

were early settlers of the county west of Purdy. Joseph McCann, who resided for many years in Purdy, where he died, was a well known business man, and was very popular. He was a man of very limited education, but good business qualities, and was noted for his kindness of heart.

JUDGE JAS. F McKINNEY

was born in Fayetteville, Lincoln county, Tenn., on the first day of September, 1822. His father, the late Dr. Chas. McKinney, was a native of Wayne county, Ky. He studied his profession at Danville, Ky., and at the age of twenty years was united in marriage with Mary A. Rupell, and in 1812, with an enterprise characteristic of the old pioneer settlers, he and his young wife emigrated to Fayetteville, where he practised his profession for 40 years, and reared a family of seven children, four sons and three daughters.

His son, the Hon. J. F. McKinney, received his education at the Fayetteville Male Academy, read law with Col. Jas. Fulton (for whom he was named) three years and then applied for and received his license, and in company with his brother, Dr. Wm D. McKinney, removed in 1846 to Purdy., Tenn., to engage in the practice of his profession, where he remained until his death, which occurred on the 21st day of May, 1880.

In the month of January, 1848, he was married to J. A. A. Adams, a daughter of B. B. Adams, Esq , an old and esteemed citizen of McNairy county. In a very few years after he entered the practice ; he was recognized as a lawyer of marked ability, and more than ordinary attainments, and a man of sterling worth and integrity

Judge McKinney had some taste for literature, but the study and practice of his profession was his highest ambition, which he prosecuted with energy and success Though not an orator he had by labor and study become learned in the law, and was ever considered a wise and safe counsellor. As an attorney in preparing his cases, he did t with the view of having them stand the test and criticism of the Superior Courts, with whom he enjoyed the reputation of being a learned lawyer and courteous gentleman.

Very soon after the war he was commissioned Judge of the Circuit Court of his district, and afterwards he received the commission of chancellor, which responsible position he filled with credit to himself and the entire satisfaction of the Bar and parties litigant. At the expiration of his term of office he again resumed the practice, and entered with zeal and energy into all the arduous labor consequent to a faithful discharge of professional duties. His practice, which had for years been lucrative, now became so onerous that he was under the necessity of giving up his business, except in his own and adjacent counties.

Judge McKinney, as a jurist, made himself felt all over the State ; as an attorney he possessed the unlimited confidence of all who knew him, but more especially of the citizens of his own county, who knew him best and who can most sadly feel in his death their irreparable loss.

As remarked of him by M. H. Meeks, Esq., in his address to the Court: "As nearly as could be said about a mortal, Judge McKinney lived, moved, and had a being in the world for fifty odd years, and died without an enemy. He stood on the stormy sea of professional life for a quarter of a century, and laid his armor down, with a character for integrity and honesty, as pure and spotless as an unclouded sky. He was as kind, as sympathetic, as inoffensive and harmless as a tender hearted woman. He was a man of strong, comprehensive, original and native brain. He was a good judge of law, and when consulted for advice always told the truth. He was a liberal man in his views, and proscribed no man on account of his belief and convictions on any subject. He was a man of pure pretentions, but when you needed a friend, you invariably found one in Judge McKinney. He gave more advice and did more actual service in his profession free of charge than any man of his ability—he was the people's friend. And to honesty and integrity of purpose in all his business relations he added the quality of an affectionate husband, a kind and indulgent father and a good neighbor."

FRANCIS BEARD.

Francis Beard was born in South Carolina about the year 1795, came to Giles county, Tenn., in early manhood and married a Miss Margaret Brown. He came to McNairy county in the year 1827, where he raised a family of ten children, four boys and six girls, as follows:

George...	married	Isabel O'Nail.
William..	"	Harriett Onsley.
Allen...	"	Rebecca Maxwell.
John..	"	E. J. Dunn.

It is to be regretted that we can not give the names of his daughters, nor who they married.

He was a member of the Primative Baptist Church, and commenced preaching about the time he came to the county. He filled that position with more than ordinary ability, until about the year 1850, when he joined the F. and A. Masons, for which he was excluded from his church. He still continued to preach to large congregations, so long as he lived, and died about the year 1867, lamented by all who knew him. He had served as Justice of the Peace in the county for eighteen years, was Collector of the State and county revenue for two years, superintended the Standard of Weights and Measures for two or three years, and was in every sense of the word a good man.

JAMES WARREN.

The McCULLER FAMILY.

Alexander McCuller, Sr., and his wife, were natives of Ireland. He came to this country before the Declaration of Independence (date not known), located in the Georgia colony, was a soldier of the Revolutionary War, raised a family of eight children— five sons and three daughters:

Sons—

John...	married	Katharine Magee.
David...	"	Elizabeth Haden.
Alexander....................................	"	Hannah Box.
Isaac..	"	Sophia Lewis.
William.......................................	"	Sarah Lewis.

Daughters—

Peggy ....married Alexander McCuller (a cousin.)
Polly.. " Mathew Marshall.
Jennie... " John Woods.

They all came to McNairy county about the year 1826, located west of Purdy. Their offsprings are numerous, and many of them are yet in the county in the third and fourth generation. Alexander, Jr., is the only one of the old stock now living in the county, and is more than eighty years old. In the main they were famed for good morals and industry. They were all farmers with abundant success and prosperity. Their religious creed was Presbyterians. Their political creed was of the Henry Clay kind ; their opinions once formed were sure and steadfast.

LEWIS B. CARTER

was born in South Carolina in the year 1803, married Lucinda Anderson in 1825, came to McNairy county in 1828, located 1½ miles southwest from Purdy, where they raised a family of six children— four sons and two daughters.

Sons—

William..married Clementine Graham.
John .... " Laura Janes.
L. B., Jr.. " Edaline Janes.
Marshall N.. " Francis Simpson.

Daughters—

Nancy... " R. J. Walker.
Sabiah.. " Stanford Sanders, Jr.

Their offsprings are but few.

Their occupation, farming, with reasonable success, always prompt to meet obligations. Politically they were Whigs. L. B., Sr., now in his 79th year, is living five miles south of Purdy, and able to look after some business.

JOHN AND JONATHAN WALSH

were brothers and natives of Wilks county, N. C. They married in that State. John's wife was Elizabeth Allen ; Jonathan's wife was Winaford Kirby (date of birth and marriage not known.) They came to McNairy in the year 1827, located in the north part of the county when a wilderness. Lands in that day were entered and held by occupancy. They were men of industry and energy, and soon opened good farms and had abundant success in raising their families and educating them the best that could be done at that early day. The old men lived to a ripe old age, died, and were buried in this county.

Their children were generally successful in their vocations, some farmers, some merchants, &c. Many of them are dead, others scattered in different States. The only one now in the county is Mrs. W. D. Jopling.

John's family consisted of seven children— six sons and a daughter, as follows :

Sons—

William C...married Harriett Spencer.
John died in early manhood.
Madison .... " Martha Johnson.

Thomas..married Katharine Kirby.
Jefferson never married.
Jesse..   "   Jennie Ingraham.

This family were in religious persuasion Methodists, and in political opinions divided.

Daughter—

Nancy..in irried A. M. Burton.

Jonathan's family consisted of ten children, six sons and four daughters, as follows :

Sons—

Henderson...married Evaline Harrison.
William K...   "   Telitha Anderson.
T. W. never married.
John L...   "   Martha Murchison.
J. F...   "   Elmira Rogers.
E. T...   "   Virginia Kincaid.

Daughters—

Elvire..   "   Spencer Holbert.
Sarah..   "   Council Mayo.
Julia...   "   W. D. Jopling.
Mary..   "   R. G. Raney.

This family in the main were Presbyterians, and, as the others, in politics, they were divided.   J. W.

ROBERT GHARTON SIMONTON

moved from Overton county to Jackson, Tenn , in 1824 or 1825. In the latter year he married Mary R., the eldest daughter of Major Charles Sevier. After his marriage he moved to Purdy. They had eight children, six of whom lived to maturity, and of whom three are now living, to-wit, Mrs. Margaret A. Hammond, of Jackson, Tenn., Adam and James Simonton.

In 1848, Mr. Simonton removed to Jefferson City, Mio., where he remained until 1851, when he went to California with his two eldest sons, Robert and Adam. Mr. Simonton died at Placerville, Cal., in 1861, aged 64 years. His wife died at Jefferson City, in 1852. The oldest child, Mrs. Keziah Farmer, died in California in 1858, Robert was drowned in 1853, Adam and James still live in California.
                                                              M. A. H.

DUKE—PRICE—TURNER.

Mrs. Judith N. Duke, with her son, Fountain P. Duke, and sons-in-law, Col. M. A. Trice, R. C. Turner, Thos. D. Duke, and Wm. A. Price, moved from Louisa county, Va., to McNairy county in the fall of 1834, and settled on Rose Creek, in the western portion of the county. The entire family remained in the county up to 1850, Col. Trice being the first to remove. He (Trice) was twice elected to the Legislature upon the old Whig Ticket, and in 1850 removed to Hardeman county, and from thence to Arkansas, where he died, leaving Mrs. E. H. Trice his widow and eight children. R. C. Turner was elected one of the magistrates of the county shortly after moving to the county, and held that position up to his death, 1852, leaving his widow, Mrs. Laura Turner, and quite a large family of children, most of whom still live in the county. Thomas D. Duke was a mechanic, and followed his trade up to date of his death. In 1856 his wife, Mrs. Elvira Duke, died very shortly after coming to the county, leaving four children—three sons and one daughter—all of whom are dead but John H. Duke, who now resides in Jackson, Tenn. W. A. Price, after remaining in the county as one of its most prosperous farmers up to 1859, removed to the State of Arkansas, where he died, leaving Mrs. Sarah Price and four children—three sons and one daughter—all of whom are living but the daughter. The Price boys are doing a very large and lucrative business at Mount Adams, on White River. We now come to speak of Fountain P Duke, the only son of Mrs. Judith N. Duke, who, as before mentioned, moved from Virginia with his mother in 1834. He was married in 1836 to Miss Kitty Price, and embarked in the mercantile business at Camden, or Rose Creek, in McNairy, and at same time kept up his farming interest. He continued up to 1861 at the above named place and had accumulated quite a nice little fortune. He removed with his own family and his mother to Arkansas in the spring of 1861, and settled on White River. His mother died in October, 1863, at the advanced age of 76 years, and Fountain P. Duke died while on a trip to Louisville, Ky., to purchase a stock of merchandise in the fall of 1876. Mrs. Kitty Duke and children are living at the place settled by them on White River, at which place they are engaged in planting.   T. H. D.

CHAPTER VII.

History of the Presbyterian Church of Bethel—Sketches of the Families of Joshua Ferguson, Charles H. Dorion, Sr., Thomas W. Melugin, Samuel D. Pace, John L. Wilkinson, Thomas Prather, Stovall, John Rains, Allen Sweat, D. Hill, Sr., James M Huggins, John Hamin, A. Houston, Samuel Chambers.

PRESBYTERIAN CHURCH OF BETHEL.

Bethel Church, situated in McNairy county, Tenn., was organized by Rev. John Gillespie, on the 7th day of September, 1828.

It consisted of 11 members, as follows :

Alexander McCullar,	Jane McCullar,
George Kidd,	Ann Kidd,
Wm. B. Wilson,	Lydia Wilson,
John Gilliam,	Rosanna Gilliam,
Alex M. Brown,	Nancy Brown,

Mary Houdon.

Alexander McCullar, Geo. Kidd, W. B. Wilson, John Gilliam, and A. M. Brown were elected and ordained ruling elders.

Mr. Gillespie preached a portion of his time to the infant church. With what degree of success his ministry was attended there is no record. But there were additions to the church at various times, and it seemed to do well and promised to prosper for a few years. But a proselyting spirit from another branch of the church broke in upon it, and well nigh swallowed it up.

After the Rev. Mr. Gillespie ceased his labors among them, the Rev. John L. Sloan ministered to them for two or three years. His services were discontinued in 1836. The Church was then vacant, with only an occasional supply ; until the spring of 1840. At that time Rev H. M. Kerr commenced preac. ing to them regularly.

The FERGUSON FAMILY.

Joshua Ferguson was long a citizen of McNairy county, settling in the Second Civil District, on the water of Mosses Creek, soon after the county was properly organized, and living there until his death, near fifty years afterwards. He was a son of James Ferguson, who came to Tennessee from South Carolina, and settled in Warren county, Tenn. James Ferguson was in the American army in the Revolutionary War. The Ferguson family were related to Col. Ferguson, who fell on the battle of Kings Mountain, fighting gallantly for the British cause.

Joshua Ferguson was a farmer by occupation. He was a soldier in the war of 1812 to 1814, which is popularly known as Jackson's war. He was under General Coffer, and participated at the battle of the "Horse Shoe." He was at New Orleans, but was not in the battle.

While quite a young man he lived awhile among the Indians, and "plowed and worked on the farm for an Indian family," and while staying there an Indian maiden fell in love with him and managed to get him unwillingly to promise to mary her. She would roast potatoes and carry to him in the field. But when she had invited the neighboring Indians to the wedding, and he saw them from the field gathering around the wigwam to witness his marriage, he mounted his horse and left the settlements.

He lived in Warren county and married Mary Herring there, and afterwards moved to McNairy county, raised a large family and lived to be 86 or 87 years old. He was an ideal farmer, and was always in politics an "Old Line Whig." He counselled against secession, and was always a Union man during the War of the Rebellion. He was a great reader of the Bible, never held to any specific views as to christianity, was never a member of any church nor of any secret society, was a great lover of the Bible and a moral and honest man. He died in the year 1872, and was buried at Sulphur Springs Graveyard, surrounded by friends and relatives, who had known him long.

The DORION FAMILY.

Charles H. Dorion, Sr., was born in the parish of l'Assumption, Lower Canada, on the 10th day of April, 1801. He came to Tennessee in 1825, and at Calhoun, McMinn county, on December 17th, 1825, was married to Hannah Sanders, who was a member of the Sanders family of McNairy county, mentioned in this book. In 1832 he moved to McNairy county, and settled at Adamsville, in the western part of the county. He entered into business here, which he continued until some time in 1835, when he removed to Purdy. He remained a citizen of Purdy until October, 1848, when he removed with his family to Bolivar, Hardeman county, where he died the 7th of March, 1870. Mrs. Dorion survived him until the 16th of September, 1875, when she died, and was buried by his side in the graveyard at Bolivar.

The children of the family were two sons— Charles H. Dorion, Jr., and W. C. Dorion. Charles went to California in 1849 or 1850, and after spending a year or more there in mining, returned to Tennessee. He settled in Memphis afterwards, and married Miss Ellen Morrison, and went into business as a cotton and commission merchant, in which he was quite successful. He was born in Calhoun, Tenn., November 12th, 1831, and died in Memphis June 1st, 1871. He was a schoolmate and classmate of the author of this book, and was in all respects a man of admirable character.

W. C. Dorion, the younger son, was born at Purdy the 27th of June, 1838. He now resides at Bolivar, Tenn., is (at this writing) unmarried. He has held the responsible office of clerk of the County Court of Hardeman county for twelve years or more, and has discharged the duties to the satisfaction of his people.

Mrs. Dorion, the mother of Charles and Willoughby, was a woman of great beauty, and noted for her charity. The elder Dorion was a man of impulse and warm temperament, fond of his family, charitable to the poor, and upright and honest in all his dealings.

The MELUGIN FAMILY.

Thos. W. Melugin came to Purdy at an early time after the settlement of the county. His eldest son, Wm. Washington, went to California in 1850, but died in a few years. The next son, James, died at an early age of dropsy. The eldest daughter, Elizabeth, married twice. The second daughter, Mary Ann (Mrs. Riddle) is now living in Columbia, Tenn. The youngest daughter, Louisa, died at an early age.

Mr. Melugin was the most popular man among the boys in Purdy, during his day, being always ready to help them in their sports. Both he and his wife were charitable and highly respected people.

The PACE FAMILY.

Samuel D. Pace was an early settler in Purdy. He came from Georgia. He was a tailor by trade but inclined to be a literary man, and indulged a great deal in writing *poetry* (?) He was an enthusiastic Whig in politics, and a leader in Whig demonstrations on public occasions.

His eldest son, John, a promising young man, died early. Samuel, the second son, died also at an early age. There were four daughters in the family.

The WILKINSON FAMILY.

BY C. F. W.

John L. Wilkinson married Martha W. Wynne, in Wilson county, Tenn, March 20th, 1828, and moved from there soon after to Purdy, Tenn. George Wilkinson was born December 28th, 1828, I think in Purdy. I think my father was one of the first settlers of Purdy. He was a merchant tailor. I think all six of his children were born in Purdy. He lived there for many years, and was said to be a good man, a strict member of the Methodist church. My mother was also a member of the Methodist church 47 years. I have often heard my mother since my father's death, speak of old John McFerrin, and many other old preachers that once sheltered under my father's roof, in time of big camp meetings and revivals. My father once owned the old Wilson Biggs Place, which stands on the road leading east of Purdy. The old mansion yet stands with its moss covered roof.

After many years in Purdy, my father started to move to Texas, and on his way he and my oldest sister Almeda died. I believe they died in 1845 or 1846, in Shelby county, Tenn., and were buried near Green Bottom. After their death my mother with five little children moved back to Purdy. George was the oldest, about 14 years old then. My mother worked hard day and night for her children; sent me to school every chance, mostly to free schools. George Wilkinson, after he became of age, went to Mexico, returned from there, stayed in Purdy a few years, and then went to California; died in Stockton, Cal., and was buried in Sacramento City. John L. Wilkinson was born January 7th, 1845, and died in 1845. Martha W. Wilkinson was born April 18, 1810, and died in Bolivar, Tenn., the 25th day of July, 1871. R. C. Wilkinson was born November 9, 1836, died April 19, 1871. Bettie married in Bolivar, Tenn., to Booker B. Hodges, of Virginia, and after his death married John M. Mitchell. She had three children by Mitchell— two girls and a boy. Some ten or fifteen years after my father's death my mother married in Purdy Henry Swann, of Virginia. Col. Henry Swann was once editor of the Jackson Whig. She had two children by Mr. Swann; the oldest, Mollie, married A. P. Piller, in Bolivar; the boy, Booker, or George Booker;

died at Grand Junction with yellow fever February 19, 1878. He was about 21 years old, a telegraph operator and a nice and good boy.

Mrs. Wilkinson still lived in Purdy after her son George went to California with her three boys, ———— ———— ; though we soon left and went in the Confederate Army. We lived in Purdy until after the surrender, and then moved to Bolivar, Tenn. P. F. Wilkinson, R. P. Wilkinson and Bettie Mitchell are the only three remaining children of John L. Wilkinson's family. P. F. Wilkinson was married to L. B. Moon September 11, 1865, in Purdy, Tenn. He had two children ; only one living, about 15 years old—Edgar Hodges. Cub Wilkinson was born March 28, 1842. Bettie Mitchell was born May 8, 1834 Jack Wilkinson was married to Sallie P. Moon January 5, 1870, at Camden, Tenn. C. F. Wilkinson married at the older Fountain Duke Place a daughter of W. C Moon.

P. F. WILKINSON.

The PRATHER FAMILY.

Thomas Prather, (his wife was Rachel Jeanes,) an early settler in McNairy county, came from Lawrence district, South Carolina, and located in the south part of this county. Their children were—

Sons—

Brice..	who married	Martha Driver.
William..	"	Unity Garrett
Thomas	"	Hariett Sears

Daughters—

Nancy	"	John Ray
Mary...	"	William Jacks
Jane..	"	William Grant.
Elizabeth	"	Josiah Jeanes
Rachel..	"	William Raimer

All of their children (except Mary Jacks) raised families in McNairy county and quite a number of their descendents remain here, and are generally successful farmers. They died some years since at an advanced age (dates not remembered)

The STOVALL FAMILY.

The Stovall family have been residents of McNairy county for many years, coming from Middle Tennessee. Their remotest ancestors, of whom they have any account, was Bartholomew Stovall, who was born May 15th, 1755. He was in the Revolutionary War, and took part in the battle of King's Mountain, under Col. Williams. He was one among the early settlers of Davidson county, was in the Frontier Fort at Nashville, then known as "French Lick," and while living there and protecting themselves in the fort, two of his boys, mere children, wandered too far from the fort "hunting cows," and were slain by the Indians. He had married Agnes Nolew, and raised a family, and after her death he was again married to Mary Ham, who was born May 18, 1753. He died September 6, 1829. George Prior Stovall was a son of Bartholomew Stovall, and was known to many citizens of McNairy county. He was born in the year 1797, and lived near where his father settled, in Middle Tennessee, until some time after he had married Elizabeth Shull, and several children were born unto them; among the number John M. Stovall and W. W. Stovall, who were afterwards well known in McNairy county. The family emigrated from Middle Tennessee in about the year 1827, first settling in Madison county, at the then village of Jackson. Moving from there in a few years afterwards, they settled in McNairy county, in the Second District, on Mosses Creek, and raised a large family. He was a poor man, and never accumulated much property, but succeeded in educating his children above the average at that time. In politics he was a strenuous Whig; he believed strong in maintaining the unity of the nation and the perpetuation of our institutions. He died at the place where he had lived for many years; the place is now known as the "old Stovall place." Leaving Elisabeth a widow with several children to care for and educate, she did well her duty, living most of her time with John M. Stovall, who aided her in maintaining herself and family. Elizabeth Stovall was born November, 1800 married January 29, 1818, and died at the residence of Nancy E. Stovall on the 27th day of March, 1878. John Milton Stovall was born July 20, 1825, came to this county when a mere boy; married Nancy E. Ferguson on December 16th, 1846. Soon after his father's death he quit farming and moved to Springfield, Mo, engaging in house carpentering, but he returned to McNairy again within twelve months to help care for and provide for his widowed mother and family, which charge he met like a hero, though he was a very poor man, so far as property was concerned. In 1855 he moved to Purdy, then a flourishing town of several hundred inhabitants. Here he worked some time at the carpenter trade, and also kept grocery, run a livery stable, &c.; he did some work on the Purdy college In politics he was always a Whig, and was once the Whig candidate for Register against Maj. Benjamin Wright; his party being in the minority, he was defeated by a slight majority. At the outbreak of the war he was opposed to secession and in favor of the Union. But when Tennessee, his native State, seceded, he sided with her afterwards and twice enlisted in the Confederate Army. He raised a company of volunteers, and was elected captain, but was never received in the service on account of the scarcity then of arms and provisions; he did not become a soldier, but went to farming to support his family. After the war he engaged in merchandising, as he had been immediately preceding the war. He studied law after the war and was admitted to the Bar as a practising attorney on the day of   1867. At his death he was an attorney for the Mobile and Ohio Railroad, having acted in that capacity for some time previous. He died in the town of Bethel Springs, on the 28th day of November, 1870, where he had lived for some time previous. He left a large family, but few of whom were grown. Among his children that were well known in McNairy, county, was David Jerome Stovall, who was born on the 21st day of April, 1851. He was very apt at study and soon procured a good education and studied telegraphy. He opened the first telegraph office at the now flourishing town of Henderson, Madison county. He held the position of railroad agent and operator at Kenton, at Troy station, and at Bethel; was at the time of his death railroad agent and operator, and express agent at Bethel, getting a good salary, having the utmost confidence of his employers and the public. He had a brilliant mind and doubtless would have attained distinction had he have lived. He originated the idea of joining the interests of Falcon and Bethel in an effort to move the county seat to the railroad. He died greatly lamented on the 4th day of August, 1876.

The RAINS FAMILY

came to McNairy county in 1826.   John Rains married Ann Gavin in 1798.   Their children were—

Sons—

William	married	Elizabeth Etter.
John	"	Jane Hammer.
James	"	Elizabeth Hughes.
Robert	"	Rebecca Cattangame.
Hugh G.	"	Margaret McCaron.

Daughters—

Elizabeth	"	Jacob Mace.
Nancy	"	Robert Luttrell.
Lucinda	"	John A. McAlpin.
Louisa	"	James Warren.

The elder Rains married in Randolph county, N. C.   They located three miles south of Purdy.   All their children, except Elizabeth Mace, raised large families in the county, and their offsprings at their death numbered (in grand and great-grand children) more than one hundred ; many of them are yet living in the county.   John Rains died in 1858, supposed to be 80 years old (no date of birth ;) his widow died in 1864, fully up to that age.   In the main they were farmers.

ALLEN SWEAT.

Allen Sweat, who married Nancy Ivens, came from North Carolina and located in McNairy county, four miles west of Purdy, in the year 1827.   Their children were :

Sons—

William	married	Elizabeth Trupe
Dallerson	"	Jane McAlpin.
Dawson	"	Susan Hunt.
Ezekiah	"	Sally Owens.
Terrel	"	Lucy Cannon.
Hilsman	"	Peggy Murry.

Daughters—

Cyntha	"	Zedariah Ivens.
Cary	"	Alfred Pryor.
Candes	"	Ward Gray.

The HILL FAMILY.

There are many things to admire and imitate in the character of the Hill people.   In the history of the whole generation, not one ever gazed through a prison bar or brought disgrace in any manner upon the name.   They are generally happy and contented, with a determination to win.   Their education, generally, is upon an average, though it has been much neglected.   Their chief occupation is farming, and not many have ever left it to follow any other.   Their home is considered their place of retreat ; and preferring the warmth of their firesides to the leisures of the outside world, they are never happier than when surrounded by those whom they love. Being of English and Irish descent, they are well developed men and women. They are noted for their longevity. Their average duration of life is 65 years. Many have lived far beyond it—not many beneath it.

They have been citizens of McNairy ever since the first settlements; they having moved to this county in the year 1828. They came from Jefferson county, East Tennessee, and settled three miles north of Purdy, on Cypress Creek. Then McNairy presented a wild and desolate appearance. Wolves howled in the wilderness, panthers screamed in the jungle, large herds of deer grazed undisturbed on the sandy hills, while smaller game, such as squirrels and rabbits, played "bast" along the mossy streams. There was nothing of a civilized nature to be seen. Purdy, itself, only contained a few huts, and a rude log court house. There were no churches, no mills, and in fact, nothing that denoted an upward tendency; but, however, they found such land as best suited them, and, as was the custom then they were contented, (notwithstanding the deficiencies,) to wear patched clothes, and to hope for a better future.

The first mill that was erected in the settlement was built by Anthony Street on Cypress, on what is now known as the McCallum place. Some of the old debris is yet visible. The first church and school house was built near Cypress, at what is now known as Plunk's mills, in 1830. The first school was taught by Daniel Griffin. It was composed of students from all the surrounding settlements within ten miles. Then it was not considered a hardship to go ten miles to school; but now it is rather a difficulty for the boys to go one fourth of a mile. Some of the leading men, in McNairy to-day, were educated at this school. In the same, year, and at the same place, a church was organized under the management of the Primitive Baptists, Franklin Beard acting as pastor. This settlement, known to-day as the Hill settlement, was among the largest then in the county. It was composed of old man Daniel Hill, Sr., and his eight sons and families, together with his sons-in-law, Isaiah Coffman, Thomas Griffin, and their families, and old Ben Walker, William Beatty, Samuel Houston, the Wilson and Rankin families.

The old generation has passed away, leaving their work in the hands of their children, which number seventy-five, now living in McNairy. Great changes have taken place since then. Instead of carrying our cotton to Memphis, (as was the custom then,) we find a market at home. The new age has brought many revolutions. The old one was buried in the "sweet long ago." The future opens her fields for improvement.   LaFayette Hill.

The HUGGINS FAMILY.

James M. Huggins was born in Buncombe county, State of N. C., on the 27th day of May, 1801, and moved to McNairy county in the year 1839, and settled in the southern part of the county. He was married in 1823 to Elizabeth Robertson, in Lauderdale county, State of Alabama. They had four children—three boys and one girl: Leroy M. Huggins, now residing at Corinth; John S. Huggins, McNairy county; J. L. Huggins, Corinth, Miss.; Elizabeth Cates, Kossuth, Miss., wife of R. C. Cates, son of Pleasant Cates, formerly of Purdy.

The HAMM FAMILY.

John Hamm, Sr., was born in South Carolina, and was 16 years old at the commencement of the Revolutionary War ; served four years in the war. At the close of the war he married Phoebe Blasengame, and moved to Kentucky and shared the Indian troubles in that State, then moved to Middle Tennessee, lived some time there and, in 1826, moved to McNairy county and lived there until his death, which occurred in the year 1835. His wife survived him twenty years.

They had eleven children, most of whom moved to this county in the years 1826 and 1827. Their names were as follows: Mary Flat, Nancy McBride, Blasengame Hamm, James Hamm, Jacob Hamm, Thomas P. Hamm, John Hamm; the balance remained in Lauderdale county, Alabama. Thomas P. Hamm, my father, was born in the State of Kentucky in 1798, and in 1818 married Tabitha Huggins, who was one year his senior, and at this date is living, moved to the county in 1826, settled on Muddy Creek, and shared all the hardships and trials incident in the settlement of a new country. His children's names are as follows: Jacob, Elizabeth, Phoebe, John M., Nancy, Sarah Benton, James M., Philip, Thomas J., Jane, Mary and Eliza; the following are the only survivors of the grave: John M. Hamm, Phoebe Fisher, Sarah Black, Nancy Fields, and James M. Hamm, Thomas P. Hamm died 1856.

The HOUSTON FAMILY.

Arch. Houston was born in the State of Pennsylvania, served through the Revolutionary War, and married Rosanna Cunningham, and at an early day moved to Kentucky, and two of his children were born in a fort. He moved to Middle Tennessee, lived there a few years and moved to McNairy county in 1822, lived in said county until his death, which occurred in the year 1837. The following are the names of his children : James, Nancy, Jane, John, Archibald, Rebecca, Robert C., Cyntha, David, and Andrew. They married as follows:

Sons—

James Houston	married in La. (name not known).
Archibald	" Stephenson.
R. C. Houston	" Rebecca Chambers.
David Houston	" Harriet Eleander.
Andrew Houston	" Emily Barnhill.

Daughters—

Nancy	"
Jane	" Thomas.
Rebecca	" John Chambers.
Cyntha	" Henry Kirkland.

Archibald Houston's family are all dead but Andrew, who lives in Texas.

R. C. Houston was born in Kentucky in 1799, moved to this county in 1822. Soon after married Rebecca Chambers before this county was organized; he had to go to Savannah to have the rights of matrimony solemnized. He with a number of other honest men knew what it was to contend with horse thieves as well as wild beasts. His children's names are as follows: Nancy, who died 6 years old ; John, who died in infancy; Elizabeth J.; Archibald K.; Lucretia, died in infancy ; Cyntha A ; Rosannah, who died in infancy

Robert S., James T., all married as follows: Elizabeth J. married John M. Hamm; Cyntha A. married James M. Hamm; Robert S. married Syrena Michel; James T. married, first, Margaret Meeks, lived with her until they had three children and she died; he married Josephine Michel. Robert C. Houston lived in this county 44 years, and in the year 1866 departed this life.

The CHAMBERS FAMILY.

Samuel Chambers was born in South Carolina, in the year 1784. At an early day he moved to Middle Tennessee and married Nancy Mackey, and in 1822 moved to McNairy county, settled on what is called Chambers Creek, in the south part of this county, and lived in said county until his death, which occurred in 1858. His first wife died in 1839, and he married a widow, Watson, but survived her a few years. His children's names are as fol.ows: John, Rebecca, Anna, Thomas, Elizabeth, Mary, Samuel, and married as follows: John Chambers married Rebecca Houston, Rebecca Chambers married R. C. Houston, Anna Chambers married Jefferson Eclam, Thomas Chambers married Elizabeth Barnhill, Elizabeth Chambers married John N. Barnhill, Mary Chambers married K. C. Ribhard, Samuel Chambers married Sarah Arnold.

John Chambers was born 1798, in South Carolina, and was brought to Middle Tennessee at an early day; came to McNairy in 1820; in the latter part of winter he went back to Middle Tennessee (1821) and married Rebecca Houston, and first settled on Owl Creek, afterwards on Chambers Creek, in the south part of this county; lived in said county until his death, which occurred in 1857. His children's names are as follows: C. L. Chambers, Lucretia, and Lavina, who married as follows: C. L. Chambers married Francis Atkins, Lucretia married O. L. Meeks, Lavinia married W. C. Meeks. John Chambers' children are all dead but one, whose name is C. L. Chambers.

B. Wright

CHAPTER VIII.

Sketches of Benjamin Wright, Martha Ann Wright, Harwell, Richard S. and Rufus S.; Marcus J. Wright, Jno. V. Wright, Elizabeth Crump, Wm. S. Wisdom, D. M. Wisdom, Public Meeting at Purdy on the Death of Wm. S. Wisdom, Mrs. Celia S. Wisdom, James Reed, P. H. Braden, I. F. Huddleston, Joseph L. Braden, Maclin Cross, Alphonso, John B. and Richard Cross; Jno. V. Wright, Richard S. Harwell, Jacob Jackson, " The Newberrys," Dr. R. W. Crump.

BENJAMIN WRIGHT.

As will be seen in a former chapter, Benjamin Wright was one of the early settlers of the county. He was born at or near Savannah, Ga., on the 2d of April, in the year 1784. His father, Capt. John Wright, commanded a company in the Revolutionary army, in what was known as the Georgia Line. Sir James Wright, the Colonial Governor, who espoused the British cause, and returned to England, was a member of a collateral branch of the family. Major Wright's mother moved to Sumner county, Tenn., after the death of her husband. There was another son named Byrd Wright, who died without having married. By a second marriage of Maj. Wright's mother there were three other children, a son and two daughters.

Maj. Wright was appointed a lieutenant in the United States army by President Madison, and was afterwards attached to the 39th Regiment of Infantry, commanded by Col. Williams, of Knoxville. He distinguished himself for gallantry at the battle of the Horse Shoe, and received several promotions, reaching eventually to a field officer. I give an extract from a letter written to me by the late Col. Charles D. McLean, who was an old an intimate friend of the subject of this sketch :

" I have hastily endeavored to throw into shape my early recollections of your venerable father, which I hope will prove of interest to yourself and family, with the only misgiving that my memory may fail me in relation to many incidents worthy of notice. Soon after the declaration of war by the United States against Great Britain, in June, 1812, Benjamin Wright was appointed a lieutenant in the army by President Madison, and was attached to the 39th Regiment of Infantry, commanded by Col. John Williams, of Knoxville. He was very soon thereafter detailed for the recruiting service, in which he was very successful in the country around Nashville, Gallatin, and Lebanon. About this time he was married to Miss Lewis, of Sumner county, Tenn., a most amiable and accomplished lady, who lived only a few years after the close of the war.

" Upon the breaking out of the Creek War, in the fall of 1818, the 39th Regiment was ordered to reinforce Gen. Jackson, who had fought the Indians in several engagements with Coffee's brigade, and other Tennesseans. They were brought into active service at the battle of the Horse Shoe, nearly the whole of Jackson's army at the time being from Tennessee.

" Lieut.-Col. Samuel P. Montgomery, of the 39th Regiment, led the charge on the breast-works at the Horse Shoe, and was killed on the ramparts.

" He was only a few paces in front of Lieut. Wright, who, seeing his leader fall, cried out " Avenge your leader," and led the charge. The charge was made in gallant style by our troops. Gen. Samuel Houston was a lieutenant in the 39th Regiment, and was wounded in the arm at this battle by a musket ball. * * * Maj. Charles Sevier, an old citizen of Jackson, Tenn., was near Lieut. Wright when storming the Indian fortification. He then lived in Overton county, but emigrated to Madison county in 1822.

" I have frequently been present and witnessed meetings between these old veterans, whose war memories they delighted to rehearse. Major (or Colonel) Wright was a man of powerful frame, upwards of six feet high, straight as an Indian, and as a business man had few equals and no superiors.

" In 1823 he married Mrs. Martha Ann Harwell (your mother) at the residence of Col. Stokeley Hays, in Jackson, Tenn., and from thence to his death resided in Purdy, McNairy county.

" When troops were called for by President Polk for the Mexican war your father volunteered as a private soldier. * * * * "

Maj. Wright had two children by his first marriage, Mrs. Francis Bracken, of Holly Springs, now dead, and Charles L. B. Wright, who was accidentally drowned at Memphis.

Maj. Wright was a soldier in the Mexican war, and contracted disease there from which he never recovered. He died in Purdy January 30, 1860.

MARTHA ANN WRIGHT.

Mrs. Martha Ann Wright was born in Dinwiddie county, Virginia. Her first husband was Herbert Harwell, by whom she had five children. Richard S. Harwell, of Purdy, Tenn ; Dr. Rufus S. Harwell, of Arkansas ; Littleton Harwell, dead ; Amanda Adams, (widow of Burnell B. Adams), of Corinth, Miss., and Julia Harwell, who died in Purdy in 1824, and was the first person buried in the old grave yard, near Purdy. Mrs. Wright had by her second marriage three children, Hon. John V. Wright, of Columbia, Tenn.; Mrs. Elizabeth Crump, now dead, and Marcus J. Wright. She died at Purdy February 27, 1852.

The following is an extract from an obituary notice written by the Rev. A. A. Saunders on the death of Mrs. Martha Ann Wright :

* * * "The deceased was a native of Dinwiddie county, Va., and was in her 66th year at the time of her death. Her maiden name was Hicks. She was twice married; first to Herbert Harwell, of her native county, by whom she had three sons : Littleton W. J. Harwell, who died in 1838 ; Richard S. Harwell, Esq., a merchant of this place, and Dr. Rufus S. Harwell, of Ouachila county, Arkansas, and three daughters, Mrs. Amanda B. Adams, of Corinth, Miss., and Elvira and Julia, both long since passed to the spirit land. * * * *
Her second marriage was with Major Benjamin Wright, of the U. S. A., then residing in Middle Tennessee. Two sons, the Hon. John V. Wright, present member of Congress from the Seventh Congressional District of Tennessee, and Marcus J. Wright, Esq., Clerk of the Common Law and Chancery Court of Memphis—and one daughter, Elizabeth, the deceased wife of Doctor Charles C. Crump, of Middle Tennessee * * Maj. Wright at an early day removed from Middle Tennessee to Jackson, and thence to Purdy. * * * Here the deceased had lived for more than thirty years, and had passed through all of the perplexities

Martha A. Wright.

and trials incident to newly settled villages. She was one of the Old Dominion's most intelligent and cultured daughters, gifted beyond measure with colloquial powers and pleasantry. She always made her visitors feel the charm of her society. She was devotedly attached to her friends, but she had to feel that the objects numbered as such, were worthy, and her discrimination was so clear that she was scarcely ever deceived. It is believed that but few mothers ever had more confidence in the integrity and uprightness of their children, or higher hopes of their eminence and prosperity, and it is pleasing to know that she had just cause to be proud of several of them.

"In her last sickness she expressed her readiness and preparation for the solemn journey before her.   *   *   She retained her reason to the last, and on Sabbath evening she quietly bade adieu to earth and entered upon an everlasting existence."

SKETCH OF BENJAMIN WRIGHT.

BY COL. DEW M. WISDOM.

The writer has a distinct recollection of Benjamin Wright. In his day, perhaps, the most popular man in McNairy county, and his popularity with all classes and all parties was due to an unending geniality that never forsook him. In politics he was a Jeffersonian Democrat "without variableness or shadow of turning," and one of those reliable followers of "Old Hickory," who, if he did not "vote early," never failed to vote for that illustrious Chieftain as *often* as his name was presented to the suffrages of the people. In McNairy county the strong tide of Jacksonism swept down every thing before its resistless current, and, if I am not mistaken, as the race between him and John Q. Adams, only two men in that county dared to vote against Jackson—one of whom was James Reed, always either a Federalist or Whig, was openly rebuked at the poles, and the other voter fared even worse at the hands of an outraged democracy. Benjamin Wright distinguished himself at the battle of Horse Shoe Bend, and in that campaign won the respect, confidence and esteem of Gen. Sam Houston, which he retained to his dying day. I saw these gallant men meet in 1352 at the old Kincaid Hotel in Purdy. Houston was returning to Texas from Washington City. Years before he had, on account of domestic troubles, quit Tennessee under a cloud, but he returned with an "Empire at his back." When did prodigal son ever return to the parental roof with so magnificent a dowry? Both Houston and Wright were men of fine physiques, each over six feet in height, and have that military air that if it does not awe is sure to attract the beholder. It was a rare treat to hear them during the short stoppage of the stage coach recount their adventures by "flood and field," and hurriedly group together the leading points of their lives. Both were fine talkers, and before the interview ended nearly the entire population of Purdy had gathered in the bar-room, (as it was called,) drawn thither to see the hero of San Jacinto and the conquerer and savior of Santa Anna. They spoke to each other in the most affectionate and familiar manner, calling each other "Ben and Sam "—"like old acquaintances free to jest." It seems at one time Major Wright visited Texas while Houston was in the heyday of his power, and he warmly rebuked him in the above interview, because he had come back to Tennessee and neglected the opportunities that were within his grasp, and which, if improved, would have made him one of the first and most conspicuous characters of the " Lone Star State." Such was Houston's estimate of the man, and who that knew Major Wright—his courage, his generosity, his utter unselfishness—can doubt that he would have won as surely the hearts of the Texans as he did those with whom his lot was cast "till in the sere and yellow leaf" he put aside his armor, and went down unblanched to his honored grave.

One incident in Col. Wright's life stands out vividly on the canvass of memory. In his old age, long after the noon of his life had passed, he heard once more the call of his country, and volunteered as a private in the war with Mexico. He served under Scott along the very route the dauntless Spaniard had gone centuries before, and bore the privations of that campaign with characteristic fortitude. I saw him on his return home welcomed by the outpouring of every man, woman and child in Purdy and vicinage. It was an ovation more heart-felt than ever greeted the exultant entry of triumphant kings. The speech of welcome was made by Jas. F. McKinny, Esq., and it was an eloquent tribute to the brave old man, who, despite his age, and the exemptions that belong to it, had set the young men of his country a noble example, and had followed the "old flag " in the perilous ridges of battle beneath a foreign sky.

Broken in the service of his country, the people elected him again and again to the office of Register of Deeds of the county, and he discharged its duties with punctilious fidelity. No man ever kept a neater set of books. They are yet extant, and are mute, yet eloquent, memorials of his patient industry, his methodical precision and undisputed accuracy There are no blurs upon their ample pages, no evidences of haste, but every page *et literatim, et punctuatim*, bespeaks the cool collected brain that guided aright the obedient pen. While these records remain, his vindication written in almost imperishable characters as a man of business will stand intact, even if he failed to leave behind him a colossal fortune, which in this utilitarian age is too often the only test of success, and the only badge of merit.

Col. Wright was a good man by nature. His generosity was not the outgrowth of the formula of schools or creeds. Little children sought his society, and played in trusting fondness at his feet, or "climbed his knees the envied kiss to share." Strong men leaned upon him in hours of adversity, and found an "anchor both sure and steadfast." When the storm came they gathered around his commanding form for protection, as do the "beasts of the field " neath the sheltering oak when the tempest sweeps the forest and marks its pathway with havoc and destruction. Women, too, were his most ardent admirers, because they knew him to be gallant, truthful and the soul of honor. No impure word ever soiled his lips, or impure thought ever darkened his counsels. He was a Chesterfield in manners, and belonged to that old school of gentlemen that sprung up immediately subsequent to the Revolutionary period, and of whom it may be truly said, " we shall not look upon their like again." Their devotion to the gentler sex was, perhaps, unsurpassed. Jackson and Clay were types of such men, and notable examples were to be found in every county, even down as late as the outbreak of our Civil war, and " within the memory of men now living."

Col. Wright was the embodiment of what the poet calls " social eloquence," and in his conversation there sparkled ever the blaze of wit and flash of bright intelligence. To young men he was especially kind, and they were always his warmest friends and most ardent supporters. Indeed, he exhibited in his daily

Jno. C. Wright

life a ready sympathy with all classes, and both his right and his left hand were devoted to charitable uses.

He lived beyond the period allotted by the Psalmist to frail humanity, and at the very threshold of octogenarian manhood " death touched his tired heart." In the " old grave yard " the polished shaft placed there by filial hands marks the spot where his remains repose and commingle with their original elements, and on its base, in the chiseled tracery of the sculptor's art, is written in fadeless letters the story of his life. That shaft rises in full view of the small village—always to him like Sweet Auburn, the loveliest of the plain—the " native heath to his wondering feet," and it overlooks the little stream whose sunny waves were never brighter than his golden traits of character.

> " Such graves as his are pilgrim shrines,
>   Shrines to no code or creed confined,
> The Delphian vales, the Palestines,
>   The Meccas of the mind."

JACKSON, TENN., Nov. 22d, 1881.

WRIGHT—HARWELL.

A SKETCH BY JENNIE S. PERKINS.

Few more seemingly hopeless tasks were ever undertaken than the search for material out of which to make distinguished personages in the rural districts of West Tennessee half a century ago. A race of pioneers, whose forefathers had been the same for several generations, with all the mental deprivation that the name implies, gave little promise of adding much to the ranks of eminent men. Yet, as the mountain torrents sometime carry gold to the valleys below, so the tide of emigration often bore upon its bosom, even at that remote period, persons upon whom an older civilization had bestowed its culture and refinement—whose descendants possessed the element of greatness by the law of hereditary transmission.

Instances that go to prove the truth of this assertion have doubtless fallen under the observation of others ; but the facts I am about to relate are based upon the vivid impressions and recollections of my own childhood and the assured facts of maturer years.

Forty years ago, Purdy, the county-seat of McNairy county, was a small village of a few hundred inhabitants, and, although it was the business centre of the surrounding county, it seemed almost as destitute of a progressive spirit as a Bedouin trading post. It had the best schools that the section afforded ; its quota of legal and medical men educated elsewhere, and its merchants and tradesmen, some of whom were in eager pursuit of wealth ; there were also some among them who had been important actors on the stage of life elsewhere. It also had its " aristocracy " ; but all lived in an unpretentious manner, content with the beauties of surrounding nature, and the quiet elegance of their homes.

In one of its modest cottages resided Major Wright, who had been a commissioned officer, and in active service under General Andrew Jackson. His commanding person, great dignity of manners and martial bearing never failed to impress all with whom he came in contact with his superiority.

The Major's wife was a queenly woman, whose grace, beauty and intellectual gifts would have adorned any position, and made her the pride of the circle in which she moved. Richard and Rufus Harwell, her sons by a former marriage, lived with them at that period.

Richard was elegant in person and dress, and possessed a nice discrimination and excellent judgment. He followed mercantile pursuits, and was a prosperous man until the ill fortunes of war ruined his business.

Rufus was a physician, and very popular. He was the handsomer of the two, and one of the most remarkable looking men I remember to have seen.

Elizabeth, John V. and Marcus J. were the offsprings of their mother's marriage with Major Wright, and were all minors when I first saw them. The daughter was very lovely, and was married in early youth to Dr. Charles C. Crump, a man who enjoyed the respect and confidence of all who knew him. She lived to grace the society of her native town a few years, and then slowly faded out of existence.

The sons early evinced a thirst for knowledge, and both obtained a classical education—a rare acquirement for that day and time. John V. chose the legal profession, and soon entered public life, embracing the principles of the Democratic party, whose idol he became. He canvassed the Seventh Congressional District in its interest, and charmed his hearers of all shades of political opinion by his eloquence. His handsome person and winning address added greatly to the effect of his works, and led his listeners' fancy captive. He was elected by his constituents a member of Congress, the greatest compliment that had ever been paid to a native of that section.

Marcus J. was an "Old Line-Whig," and on attaining his majority went to Memphis, Tenn., to reside, and was elected Clerk of the Common Law and Chancery Court, a very honorable and remunerative position. He was gifted with sound judgment, great executive ability, and a correct literary taste, and before the late war was known as an able contributor to Southern literature.

Both brothers espoused the cause of the South. They were promoted at once, and remained in active service until John V. was called from military to civic duties in the Confederate Congress at Richmond.

Marcus J. Wright was made Brigadier General and Military Governor of Columbus, Ky., during its occupation by the Confederate forces. He was appointed on the 1st of July, 1878, by the Secretary of War, for the purpose of collecting for the use of the Government such records of the late war, (on the Confederate side) as could be obtained.

In our humble judgment no better selection could have been made; and we, in common with all native McNairyans, feel a pardonable pride in speaking of a family that was identified with the pioneer settlers of our section, and whose members are an ornament to our common country.

WILLIAM SARGENT WISDOM.

Wm. S. Wisdom was one of the oldest and the most prominent of the citizens of McNairy county. He was a man who achieved success in life, was ever the friend of the poor and deserving, and staunch defender of the widow and orphan. He died at his residence in Purdy on November, 19, 1871, in the 75th year of his age.

The writer of this article has from boyhood known Mr. Wisdom, having been reared in the village in which he has passed his life, and having in early life been the recipient of his kindness, and preserved his fast friendship up

Wm. S. Windom

to the day of his death, he now feels that it is but a labor of love to speak of him as he was, now that he "sleeps with his fathers."

Mr. Wisdom was born in Rockingham county, North Carolina, on the 14th of July, 1796; his father, James Wisdom, moved to Anderson county, East Tennessee, in 1809; in 1811 he moved to Overton county, and from there in 1820 he moved to Western Tennessee, and settled near what is now known as Henderson Station; in the following year he came to McNairy county, where the subject of of this notice resided up to the day of his death. Mr. Wisdom had but a limited education, but as it has been aptly said of another, "As Cornish diamonds are not polished by any lapidary, but are pointed and smoothed even as they are taken out of the earth," so *nature* itself was all the *art* which was used upon him.

He went to school at night and worked during the day to pay his tuition and .assist his father. Being a man of extraordinary mind, he advanced rapidly and acquired the ordinary rudiments of an English education in half the time required by most scholars with the best advantages. He afterwards taught a small school in his neighborhood, supplying the place of his former teacher, who had died. He served for some time as a deputy in the office of the county court clerk of his county, and was subsequently elected clerk. These were all the public offices he ever held; yet his personal popularity was very great, and increased up to the day of his death. He afterwards engaged in merchandise, and became one of the largest land-holders in the State. He acquired a handsome fortune, and was always foremost in works of charity and public enterprise. He was married in 1833 to Jane Anderson, by whom he had three sons and five daughters, all of whom survive him, except his wife and second son; his eldest son, Colonel D. M. Wisdom, distinguished himself as a Confederate soldier in the late war, and was the editor and proprietor for some years of the Jackson *Whig and Tribune*. His second wife, who survives him, was Mrs. Celia Shull. Both wives were excellent women, worthy of such a husband.

In domestic life he was neighborly and companionable, fond of the society of the young, and was never better pleased "than when promoting youthful pleasure by participation and encouragement;" he ever proved himself the devoted and affecinate husband and father, and the faithful and enduring friend. When in full health and surrounded by all of earth's advantages which could contribute to render his life one of happiness and pleasure, he reviewed for himself the evidences of Christianity, pondered upon its truths, felt its sacred influences, and deliberately made his decision; he deemed it of far more importance than all of regard and reverence which this world could confer. He became a member of the Christian (or Campbellite) Church, and lived and died in full faith of a happy immortality. His latter days were marked with tranquil cheerfulness. In the bosom of a family that was most dear to him, he was blessed with—

"All that should accompany old age,
As honor, love, obedience."

As an evidence of the regard had for him among the people with whom he had lived for half a century, on the day after his death a public meeting was held at the court house in his county town, attended by all classes of the community. Eloquent and feeling speeches were made; strong men wept, and old men sobbed aloud, and all felt that a friend of the poor, of the widow and orphan, had gone, and there was no one left to fill his place. Mr. Wisdom's whole heart was enlisted with the South in the late war, and while rude soldiers were quartered on him, his money and property forcibly taken from him, and even personal indignities offered him and family, he never swerved from his loyalty to his own people.

In person he was of the ordinary height, his form inclining to portliness, his hair brown, mixed with gray; his eyes gray, and full and prominent; his countenance was intelligent, and its expression mild, cheerful and benevolent, indicative of contentment and happiness, yet it showed much decision and firmness of purpose; his manners were courtly, amiable, unaffected, kind and conciliating in a high degree; his conversation was entertaining and instructive, abounding in humor and playful wit; his even and cheerful disposition rendered him the delight of he domestic circle in all the relations of which he exhibited an example worthy of imitation He drew his morals from the pure fountain of Christian ethics, and was severe only with himself, being always charitable and lenient toward others· In his transactions and intercourse with his fellowmen, his conduct was always governed by an inflexible sense of justice and integrity.

Forewarned by a long and painful illness of his approaching dissolution, he met death calmly and without fear, and

> "Gave his honors to the world again,
> His blessed part to heaven, and slept in peace."

M. J. W.

PUBLIC MEETING AT PURDY—DEATH OF WM. S. WISDOM ESQ.

On Monday, November 20th, the citizens of Purdy assembled at the court house for the purpose of paying suitable tribute of respect to the memory of W. S. Wisdom, Esq., one of the oldest and best citizens of McNairy county, who died November 19, 1871, at his residence.

The object of the meeting being explained by A. B. Person, on motion, Judge J. F. McKinney was called to the Chair, and Geo. E. Meeks appointed Secretary. A. B. Person, Jas. W. Purviance and John M. Harris were appointed by the Chair as a committee to draft resolutions of respect to the dead, and of sympathy and condolence with the bereaved kindred and friends.

While the committee were drawing up the following resolutions I. F. Huddleston, Esq., and Rev. R. M. Thompson spoke in eloquent terms of the noble traits and the great loss to the country of such a citizen. The following resolutions were submitted by Jas. W. Purviance, Esq., accompanied with appropriate and eloquents words of eulogy, and unanimously adopted:

Whereas, In the order of Nature, it has pleased the Creator of all things to remove from us our much esteemed fellow citizen, W. S. Wisdom; that we, feeling the great loss to the community by his death, do, in meeting assembled, hereby express our deep sense of his worth, by resolving,

1st. That his loss is universally felt by all the people of this community.

2d. That we highly appreciate his many virtues, and deeply deplore the loss of one who was ever a constant and dear friend to the poor, and an honor and ornament to society.

3d. That the business of the community loses a man who was always in advance of any project that would promote the welfare of the county; one that always true to his promises, and honorable in all his business transactions.

4th. That in his death his much loved wife has lost one of the noblest hus-

Celia M. Wisdom,

bands, his children an indulgent and loving father, and that our deepest sympathies are extended to them in their great afflictions.

5th. That a copy of these resolutions be sent to the wife and each of the children of the deceased, and also a copy of the same, with request that they publish, to the Jackson *Whig and Tribune*, and the Bolivar *Bulletin,*

A. B. PERSON,
JAS. W. PURVIANCE,
J. M. HARRIS,
Committee.

Geo. E. Meeks, *Secretary.*
Nov. 20th, 1871.

MRS. CELIA (SHULL) WISDOM.

Mrs. Celia Wisdom was born near Mobile, on her grandfather's plantation, where the town of Blakeley now stands, on Mobile Bay, the 14th of January, 1804. Her maiden name was Celia Sherman. She emigrated to McNairy county in the year 1824, accompanied by her mother, her step-father and two sisters, and settled at Purdy.

In 1826 she was married to Peter Shull, by whom she had two children, Calvin and Margaret, the latter of whom married John G. Combs in 1847, and died in 1863, leaving five children.

Mrs. Shull's second marriage was with Wm. S. Wisdom. She is a remarkable woman both mentally and physicially. She and Richard S. Harwell are the oldest survivors of the early settlers of McNairy county. She is a woman of large physical proportions, commanding and striking in appearance, and her intellectual qualities are fully in keeping with her physique. Her memory is most remarkable, and her conversational powers are surpassed by few. She is at this writing the oldest living person of the early settlers of the county.

Peter Shull, her first husband, came with his father, John Shull, and his brother, Nathaniel, and sister, Lean, to McNairy from Maury county at an early date. He was a partner in business with W. S. Wisdom for many years, and a fine business man, and was quite successful, leaving his family in very comfortable circumstances at the time of his death.

Nathaniel Shull and Lean, Mrs. Gilespie, are still living near Purdy.

Calvin, the olest son of Peter and Celia Shull, has been a leading and popular business man in Purdy since he was a young man. He held for some years the office of clerk of the county court. He married Mary, the eldest daughter of Wm. S. Wisdom, and has resided until very recently in Purdy. The old Wisdom mansion in Purdy, which Calvin and family and his mother resided in was recently destroyed by fire, and he has since removed to Jackson, Tenn.

SKETCH OF JAMES REED

In the past of Purdy there flourished an eccentric character by the name of James Reed, *alias* " Uncle Biddle." He was indeed *sui generis*, a *rara avis*, one of those original men in word and action, who leave their impress upon the community which holds them, and through life on account of certain traits of character attract a large share of public attention, and are rolled as a sweet morsel under the tongues of gossippers.

He was born in Maryland, near the Pennsylvania line, and brought to his Southern home much of the shrewdness, thrift and enterprise of a "regular down Easter." In early life he was a flat boatman, and carried produce, staves, &c., from Cincinnati to New Orleans, and there disposing of his boat and cargo, returned on foot through a wild and unsettled country often infested with robbers, and overrun with savages and bears, wolves and panthers.

We have been told that he made seventeen trips in succession before he abandoned so hazardous a life, and it may be proper to mention here that "Uncle Biddle" had as flat a foot as ever trod *terra firma*. It looked, indeed, as if it might have been, if not "smoothed by a scythe"—at least "leveled by a roller," and its unusual flatness was always attributed to the fact that he had reduced it to that shape by its constant use on his return trips, and he could walk with such rapidity that no horse was his match in endurance—save in the first days of his journey. He distanced everything like a horse on the "home stretch," and came victoriously stepping into Cincinnati ahead of time to the tune of forty to fifty miles per day. It is supposed that these trips were profitable to "Uncle Biddle," since he had too shrewd an eye to business to pursue any venture that did not bring forth fruit in due season, and put money in his pockets.

His ruling passion—his predominating trait—was an intense aversion to the Democratic party. If Dr. Johnson liked an honest hater, his love for "Uncle Biddle" would have exceeded all computation. He honestly believed that the removal of the deposits and the overthrow of the United States Bank was the parent cause of all the evils that afflicted the country and harrassed the people, and he hated old Hickory and the hosts that went out under his banner with an intensity that bordered on the fiercest fanaticism. He always called a Democrat a Locofoco, and no occasion, no time, and no person could so move him as to force a change of what he deemed the most expressive term of hate within his range of expletives. In the race between Jackson and Adams, Uncle Jimmie was one of the two men who voted for Adams in McNairy county, and as he neared the polls to cast his ballot, he was told by the sheriff, who received it, that whoever voted *against* Jackson was a traitor to his kind and his country. Uncle Jimmie responded in terms fully as polite, if not more emphatic—"denouncing both the allegation and the allegator," and a row seemed imminent, which, had it occurred, somebody would have been badly hurt. It took a bold man in those days to vote an open ticket against Jackson. But Uncle Jimmie was a bold man and honest one too, and would have followed his convictions to the death. I recall another incident in his career. "Uncle Biddle" took the contract to build the Court House at Purdy, and he completed the job in a workmanlike manner. He had taken a vow in his youth that he would never do another day's work after he had reached his 50th year. I mean another day of manual labor. This vow he faithfully kept. On his fiftieth birthday he laid aside his plane, and during life never cut another shaving, or smoothed another board. On the day, or about the time of the completion of the Purdy Court House, the celebrated Davy Crockett made his first appearance as a political stumper in those parts. "Uncle Biddle" had sworn by all the Gods at once, that no man should speak in or otherwise use or occupy the Temple of Justice, until it had been received by and the keys delivered up to the County Commissioners. On this point he was both "solid and unanimous." Crockett very much desired to speak in the court house, but on his first to application 'Uncle Biddle" he was met with a prompt refusal. Chagrined and mortified, as he was, still Crockett determined to try some other mode of access to the obdurate heart of Uncle Jimmie. In the night before the day of the speaking some *one* whispered unto " Uncle Biddle's " ear that Crockett was likely to overhaul Jackson and his administration, and, perhaps, ventilate " Old Hickory " generally. No sunbeam ever melted down a snow-bank more rapidly than this welcome intelligence softened the feelings of " Uncle Biddle." His heart at once relented, and the dawn of morning found the old gentleman, broom in hand, and aided by one or two assistants, sweeping out the trash, arranging seats, and doing everything to promote the comfort and convenience of the distinguished " bear hunter and politician of Tennessee." Uncle Jimmie defended himself by saying that if the court house was to be dedicated to the reformation of the public morals, he knew nothing better in a preliminary way than an anti-Jackson speech ; that in the course of time the Locofocos might fire the *last* gun, but he had given the *first* shot, and that was one point gained in a good cause, and he always contended that Crockett cumbered the ground with the killed and wounded, and that his speech was a telling and powerful effort, full of homely, yet apt illustrations, and sparkling with a flow of humor that belonged alone to Davy Crockett.

When ever there was a joint discussion between leaders of the old parties at Purdy, " Uncle Biddle " was alive, active and aggressive. He seemed to snuff the battle from afar like Job's war horse, and appeared bedecked in war paint and feathers, so to seak, and with tomahawk in hand. Woe to the un.appy knight of a Democrat that came in his pathway! It is said he never but once heard a Democratic speaker. If the Whig champion opened the discussion he was always promptly present, and usually occupied a chair, which he located near the stand, in order that no word might escape him, and that he might sit under the " very droppings of the sanctuary." When the Whig orator closed his speech—at the very instant—" Uncle Biddle " " stood not upon the order of his going, but went at once," amid the smiles and sometime illy-suppressed tones of derision on the part of his Democratic friends and neighbors. His exit on such occasions was really a dramatic performance. His step was as agile as an Indian, his face red as a bandana handkerchief, and he struck his cane upon the unoffending earth with violent energy. That cane had the most peculiar rattle I ever heard, and the recollection of it clings to me yet over the weary roll of years entombed in the unreturning past. I said he never heard but one Democratic speech. It seems that he was prevailed upon to hear a joint discussion between Coleman and Stanton, who were opposing candidates for Congress in the Memphis district, to which at that time McNairy county was attached. Stanton had the reputation of a *fair* debator, that is to say, he did not abuse his opponents, and dealt hard, but courteous blows. True to his word, " Uncle Biddle " sat through the debate. Yes, he *sat* bold upright through it; clenched his hand firmly about the head of his cane, and fixed an eye as keen and glittering as that of the " Ancient Mariner " upon Stanton, who was greeted again and again with storms of applause by his party friends. There was the usual clapping of hands, stamping of feet, and loud huzzas " outvoicing the deep mouthed sea. No doubt the very fires of hate fiercely burnt in his bosom, but he gave no sign. He sat as imperturbable as a granite shaft, and apparently heedless of the tumultous popular uproar that raged around him. When the discussion ended he left the court house, and those who saw him report the old gentleman to have been " exceeding wroth," and tradition says he filled the air with oaths tolerable to neither men nor Gods. We have heard him say that on that occasion he heard enough Locofoco lies to drown a thousand men, and that he never would again be so weak as to be caught in such a trap. It is needless to say he never attended another similar discussion.

On another occasion the writer wanted to make a short trip into one of the districts of his native county, impelled, perhaps, more to see a "bonnie lassie" than to be edified upon the tariff, or upon the records of the opposing candidates. In those days it was not always convenient to procure a horse, and hence we resorted to a little stratagem. We told "Uncle Biddle" that on such a day a celebrated Whig speaker was to orate at such a place, and that then and there a Whig club would be formed, and that I had been informed there was a need of a few battle-flags, as Judge Sneed said about the mountains of East Tennessee, to "decorate" the ceremonies; that I had a few left over from a former celebration, which I would be glad to hand over to the chairman of the committee on arrangements, provided I could get a horse to carry me to the field of action. The old gentleman furnished me a horse at his own expense, and I set out as "brave a lad as ever commission bore, to display the Whig bunting to the 'battle and the breeze.'" By some mistake the orator failed to put in an appearance, the club was not evolved from the inner conciousness of the local politicians, and the anticipated jubilation was a flat failure. I knew the old gentleman too well to return with a true report of what occurred, and so I resorted to another piece of strategy. On my return I found the old gentleman standing on tip toe eager for the fray, and ready as he always was to hear of a mighty uprising of the people in behalf of Whig candidates and measures.

I told him in substance as follows: "That whilst I did not regard Mr. B. as a great orator, that he made strong and telling points in his speech; that among other things he said that the Locofocos had charged that Henry Clay was a black-leg, a duelist, and his morals generally were bad and loose beyond utterance, and that he was, therefore, unfit to occupy the Presidential Chair once filled by a Washington. That he, Mr. B., had but one way of meeting such slanders, and that was by giving it the "lie direct," that he wished it to be distinctly understood that he had measured his words, and was *personally* responsible for them both *here* or *elsewhere*." "Uncle Biddle" was delighted at my recital of the points of the speech, and he spoke out quickly, with the old war gleam in his eye, "Do I understand you to say that he called them 'Locofocos, or d——d Locofocos? I replied, Locofocos with an epithet.

Yes, said "Uncle Biddle," and he (Mr B.) was willing to be *personally* responsible for his words. Oh, yes, said I, *personally responsible*.

And no Locofoco, said "Uncle Biddle," dared to take him up or meet his denial?

Nobody whimpered "Uncle Biddle," said I. All was as silent as the grave.

Whereat the old gentleman again assailed the earth with his cane, and said the only way, (he had always said it,) to beat Locofocos was to cram the lie down their throats, and to keep it so crammed down well. "Strong coffee" was the only medicine that a milk and cider policy was sure to end in ruin; that he was for carrying the war into Africa, &c. *Carthago est delenda* was his motto!

Having told him of the above point, like Oliver Twist, he yearned for more, and I bethought again of his eternal hatred to Jackson, and I went on to report that B. had denounced the removal of the deposits as an act of high-handed tyranny that in Europe would have cost Monarchy a crown, and that for this act he held Old Hickory up to the reprobation of mankind as a tyrant, who in history would take his place by a Nero or Caligula, and that he had destroyed the best currency the world ever saw by his overthrow of the United State Bank.

Did he say Jackson was just a tyrant, or a d—ned tyrant? said "Uncle Biddle."

If I recollect right, "Uncle Biddle," he said he was a *d—ned Locofoco tyrant*.

The old gentleman could stand no more. His cane rattled with a nervous energy; it described gyrations in the circumambient air; his whole frame shook with a wrathful kind of joy, and he directed me to write to Mr. B. at once to make an appointment at Purdy; that he had heard of his celebrated speech in the Eighth District; that he would assure him a big crowd; that Clay was certain to be elected, &c. I wrote the letter, of course, but to this date I am reasonably certain it has never been mailed, and that it never reached its destination.

With him, indeed, the "ruling passion was strong in death." He died in 1852, on the eve of the Presidential election, fully confident that Scott would sweep the country, and enter the Presidential Chair backed by a large popular majority.

A few days before his death the writer visited him, and cheered his dying hours by reading extracts from Whig newspapers. His favorite paper was the Louisville *Journal*, and he was never so happy as when hearing editorials from the pen of the gifted Prentice.

On one such visit I called his attention to a knot of gentlemen, residents of Purdy—all Democrats—who were holding a conversation near McCann's old grocery store. He viewed them a moment in sullen defiance, and asked me what was the object of the meeting. Replying that I did not know, he rallied with his old-time energy, and said: "Well, I know they are traitors, (with an epithet,) plotting against the liberties of the people. You will live to see the country, my son, wasted by war and ruin overtake you all, and the Locofocos will be at the bottom of the devilment. It has always been my belief they would ruin the country, and I die in that belief." I copied these words in an old scrap-book at the time, and their strict accuracy may be relied upon by all who reads these lines. Another trait or two, which ought perhaps to have been noticed earlier, and I shall have done this rough and hasty penciling. Before election day "Uncle Biddle" was the impersonation of aggressiveness. He wore the hypothetical coat tail of Donnybrook Fair, and was literally "spoiling for a fight." Mad himself, he always asserted that the Democrats were mad also, and by a singular and happy hallucination he drew inspirations of victory from that very fact. His constant cry was, "Boys, the Locofocos are mad; they know that defeat awaits them, and w'eve got them. But if "Uncle Biddle" had his nap up before election day, how furiously he raged when the returns came in and showed his favorite champion under an avalanche of overwhelming ballots. Then, indeed, he quit the public streets and his accustomed haunts through sheer disgust, retired to his room, and there remained a week or so like a weather-beaten vessel hauled in docks for repairs. At such a time he had no company and wanted none, and he never rallied until he had the Louisville *Journal* read over to him, which, of course, abused the Whigs for staying at home, and not having patriotism enough left to vote their principles, and two or three copies of it would usually satisfy him that there was really no *decrease* in the Whig ranks, but just a criminal negligence to vote; and also, " Uncle Biddle" had a keen nose for frauds which never failed to cut an important figure in every race that resulted in the defeat of his favorites. According to his arithmetic very few Democrats were ever honestly elected, and where he living to-day his voice would roll over the border into Mississippi, demanding a "full vote, a free ballot, and a fair count." "Uncle Biddle," (so called after Nicholas Biddle, the President, I believe of the once famous United States Bank,) bought several acres of ground, which he divided into small lots, and his purchase was known as Reed's addition to the original plat of Purdy. It, therefore, become necessary for him to make warranty deeds to purchasers, and these deeds were often drawn after the old style by Maclin Cross, Esq., the leading Democrat of McNairy county. The old gentleman procured Cross to write them, but before he would attach his signature he required that they should be read over and their correctness vouched for by the late W. S. Wisdom, a well-known Whig, whose political faith, outside of his sterling integrity, was a sufficient avouchment to " Uncle Biddle " that the calls and dimensions of the lots were set out correctly in the conveyances, and so in commercial matters even the doughty old Whig carried the leaven of his politics.

Brave old Whig cavalier! No gorganic horrors born of a craven spirit stood around your dying pillow to mock you with a lack of courage in your life work. You followed your convictions to the end, and a consciousness of this fact cheered you in your last moments, and you died as peacefully as the exultant crusader in full view of the Holy Sepulchre. You were one of those rare men who never deceived either friend or foe, and your very eccentricities constitute the best heritage you have transmitted to posterity. It may be truly said of you that " all your faults leaned to virtues," and that but one epitaph should fitly be inscribed upon your tomb: " Here lies an honest man, the noblest work of God." Even in your death you grandly rose above your time and section. You manumitted the only slave you ever owned, endowed him with a portion of your estate, and bade him hurry onward from the dark confines of slavery to the sunlit fields of freedom. I say again, brave old Whig cavalier! You have gone beyond the River to rest beneath the shade of the trees, and should some proud unconquered banner of your beloved party roll out its folds upon a sunny mount of Zion, we feel assured that you are there ready to join Jno. Quincy Adams in denouncing the charge of "bargain, intrigue and corruption " made against Henry Clay as a falsehood, even though it should emanate from omnipotence itself.

D. M. WISDOM.

The BRADEN FAMILY.

Major P. H. Braden was born in Williamson county, Tenn, February, 1800; removed to Maury county, and in the year 1822, inter-married with Margaret Lane, *nee* McEwin, of Maury county. The issue of this marriage was one son, Dr. Joseph L. Braden. She died, and he inter-married with Sally M. Johnson, of the same county. Born to them nine children, towit: Mary E., who inter-married with Col. I. F. Huddleston, March 7th, 1861; W. H., who inter-married with Martha Martin, daughter of Judge James Martin, of Harden county, Tenn.; M. J Braden, who inter-married with Jennie Bell, daughter of John Bell; Martha D., who inter-married with John W. Stumple; Sarah J., who inter-married with

Tendell Crump, son of Dr. Richard Crump, of Hardin county, Tenn; George W. who inter married with Nora Hollingsworth, daughter of Judge Hollingsworth, of Kentucky, who now lives in the city of Louisville—merchant; T. J., who intermarried with Mattie Crump, daughter of Dr. Richard Crump, of Hardin county, Tenn., and sister of Tendell Crump.

Maj. P. H. Braden died December 5, 1870, at the age of seventy, and was buried in the cemetery at Purdy, after a residence in the county of McNairy for about forty years. He was a man of fine physique, of strong mind, and was among the leading Democrats of the county during the days of the Whig and Democratic parties of anti-bellum times. Dr. Joseph L. Braden was an eminent physician of his age, but met his death untimely at the hands of Capt. Wm. Forrest in 1863 at the home of his father in Purdy; Mary E. enter-married with I. F. Huddleston, who was born in Clairborn county, East Tennessee, went to McNairy county in the year 1852, studied law, and when quite young took a high stand in his profession. Mr. Huddleston at the age of sixteen years was an officer in the war with Mexico, he and Col. Burch having organized a company in the mountains of East Tennessee, joined Col. Waterhouse's regiment, 4th Tennessee Volunteers. After the close of the late war between the States he settled down in Purdy, and has been practicing law there ever since.

The CROSS FAMILY.

Judge Maclin Cross, whose name is frequently mentioned in this book, was one of the early settlers of the county, and one of its most prominent and respected citizens.

He was the first clerk of the county court, was delegate to the Constitutional convention of 1835, was Judge of the county court, and held other places of trust, and was the acknowledged leader of the Democratic party in his county. He was a merchant and lawyer, his practice in his profession, however, was mostly office business, he seldom appearing before the courts. He married Miss Denny, a sister of Alvin Denny, a very handsome and intelligent woman. He removed after 1865 to Humboldt, where he died some time last year, nearly, if not quite, eighty years old. His eldest son, Alphonso Cross, who died a few years since, was a man of rare qualities. He was truly a man of "infinite wit and most excellent humor." He was most of his life engaged in merchandise. He was clerk and Master of the chancery court of McNairy county for many years. He raised and took into the Confederate service from McNairy county a company which formed part of the 13th Tennessee Regiment, commanded by Col. Jno. V. Wright, and subsequently by General A. J. Vaughan.

Jno. B. Cross, the second son, married a Miss Woodward, of Mississippi, and died in Arkansas a few years since. Richard, the youngest son, married a Miss Joidon, of Tennessee, and was drowned some years ago. There were three daughters, none of whom to the writer's knowledge are living.

Albert Cross, a younger brother of Judge Cross, married Miss Jane Pace, daughter of Sam D. Pace, at an early day, and removed to Texas. Emily, a sister, married Thomas Johnstone, who died in Purdy many years ago. The widows of Alphonso and Richard Cross reside at Humboldt.

JNO. V. WRIGHT,

the eldest son of Benjamin and Martha A. Wright, was born at Purdy June 28, 1828. He was once a candidate for the lower house of the General Assembly of Tennessee from McNairy county, but was defeated by one vote—the vote of his opponent. He served three terms in the Congress of the United State from the (then) Seventh District in which McNairy county is situated. He resigned his seat in 1860. In 1861 he raised the 13th Regiment of Tennessee Infantry for the Confederate Army, and commanded it as Colonel at the battle of Belmont, Mo., where he was wounded. He was soon afterwards elected to the Confederate Congress, where he served until the end of the war. He has resided for a number of years at Columbia, Tenn. He has held the offices of Judge of the Circuit, Criminal and Chancery Courts in his judicial district, and has also been several times appointed by the Governor as special judge of the Supreme Court of the State.

He was the candidate of the State Credit Democracy for Governor of the State at the election in 1880, but by reason of the division in the party, (there being two candidates,) was defeated by Governor Hawkins.

He has a leading practice at the bar of Columbia, and enjoys to a large extent the confidence and regard of the people.

RICHARD S. HARWELL.

As will be seen elsewhere, Richard S. Harwell has lived longer in McNairy county than any one now living except Mrs. Celia Shull Wisdom. He is the oldest son of Mrs. Martha Ann Wright by her first marriage.

He is a fine business man, and was a successful merchant in Purdy for many years.

In early days he was a great hunter, and enjoyed the reputation of being one of the best *shots* in the county. He still resides in Purdy.

JACOB JACKSON.

Jacob Jackson was born in North Carolina on the 10th day of April, 1796; emigrated to East Tennessee with his father; went into the war of 1812 at the age of seventeen; served one campaign; married to Mary Fillpot, who was a native of Virginia; emigrated to McNairy county, Tenn., in the year 1826; served as justice of the peace for thirty years; died September the 17th, 1880, age 84 years, 5 months and 7 days.

The NEWBERRYS.

Sarah and Isabella Newberry, familiarly called "Sally and Ibby," removed from Owl Creek, McNairy county, to Purdy in 1832, where they soon became noted for their industry and cleanliness, but especially for the "ginger-cakes and beer," which they sold as a means of support. In 1850 their brother-in-law from East Tennessee came to see them, and they returned with him.

DR. RICHARD W. CRUMP

was an eminent physician of McNairy county, and a man of extraordinary mental powers. He settled many years ago on the Tennessee river, at Crump Landing, where he died. His widow, who still survive him, is a sister of Mrs. Celia Shull Wisdom.

John W. Meeks

CHAPTER VIX.

The wood-cut picture of General John H. Meeks will be recognized by all McNairy people, old and young.

Gen. Meeks' family was of English origin. The family in this country descended from two brothers, Littleton and Nacy, who settled in South Carolina. Both of them were Baptist preachers, and were regarded as very able, as well as pious and good men. General John H. Meeks is the grandson of the eldest of these brothers, Littleton Meeks, and the son of the eldest child of his grandfather. His father moved at an early day to Georgia, and there married the eldest daughter of Capt. John Henderson, an officer in the Revolutionary army. The subject of this sketch was named John Henderson in honor of his grandfather, by whom he was taken from infancy and brought up, his mother having died soon after his birth. There were two other brothers, Thomas Harvey and Felix Grundy Meeks, both of whom died in Lincoln county, Tenn., to which county the family had moved in 1811. Gen. Meeks' father married a second time, by which marriage there were several children, among whom was Col. Orville S. Meeks, so well-known and highly respected in McNairy county. The elder Meeks moved to McNairy county in the fall of 1844, and died in March, 1877, being about ninety years of age at the time of his death. He was a man who had the universal confidence and respect of his neighbors and acquaintances, his whole life being one of good example, and strict adherence to principle. He was for fifty years a member of the old Baptist Church.

Gen. Meeks was born in Lincoln county, Tenn., on the 27th day of September, 1814, and, as before stated, was brought up by his grandfather, Capt. John Henderson, who moved to Alabama in February, 1820, from whence he moved to McNairy county in 1830, settling on Oxfords Creek, where his young grandson, with the aid of some negroes, cleared up some land and made a crop of corn. The old Captain remained at his Oxford Creek home until February 20, 1840, when he died, making John the executor of his will.

In 1836 and soon after the adoption of the Constitution of 1834, Mr Meeks was elected major of the Second Battalion of the 108th Regiment Tennessee Militia, an office in those days of great honor, but no pecuniary profit. Two years subsequently he was elected colonel of the regiment, and was afterwards elected brigadier-general. In 1840 he was appointed Deputy United States Marshall for McNairy county, and had charge of the census taken that year.

In 1843 Col. Meeks was the Democratic candidate for representative in the General Assembly from McNairy county, but was defeated by Matt. A. Trice, the

Whig candidate, by a strict party vote, the majority of the successful candidate being 14 votes.

In 1845 he was again the candidate of his party for the same position, and was defeated by his warm personal friend, James Warren, by 50 votes. He was in 1849 for the third time renominated by the Democrats, and elected by 133 votes, and re-elected in 1851 by 116 votes.

In the canvass of 1849 Col. Meeks took ground in favor of the Homestead law, and was probably the first man in the State who ever publicly advocated that just and popular measure. In 1853 the nomination was again tendered him, but he declined, and John V. Wright was nominated, and defeated by one vote—that vote being cast by his opponent. The Democrats of the senatorial district, composed of the counties of Hardeman, Hardin and McNairy, this year nominated Gen. Meeks for the State Senate, but he declined the nomination.

Gen. Meeks passed his time quietly at home up to the beginning of the war. Two of his sons entered the Confederate army, and his residence being in the neighborhood of Shiloh Church after the great battle fought there in April, 1862, he was subjected to many annoyances and losses, and would have lost his life but for the interference of Gen. Grant.

In December, 1869, he again entered public life, this time being elected by an overwhelming majority as delegate from his county to the Constitutional Convention. Since then he has devoted himself to home affairs, withdrawing entirely from political or public life. Gen. Meeks' wife was Miss Eleanor Atkins, whom he married in 1841, by whom he has a large family of children, all of whom are promising and highly respected, and some of whom occupy important places of trust. One of his sons, George L. Meeks, who married Mary McKinney, and died a few years since, was Clerk of the Circuit Court of McNairy county, and Marcus H. Meeks is the present Attorney General of the Judicial District, in which McNairy county is situated, and is a man of marked ability.

The ADAMS FAMILY.

BY T. L. A.

Jeremiah Adams was born in Dinwiddie county, Va., in 1776; moved from there to Bedford county, Va., where he was married to Elizabeth Grigg, who was born in Bedford county October 14, 1776; married in 1799. They remained in that county, where they had eleven children born to them, eight sons and three daughters, who grew up to be grown except two. One son named Richard died at the age of about 18; a daughter named Martha age about 15. Seven sons and two daughters grew up to be grown in Virginia, four of whom were married in that State, to-wit: Three sons, B. B. A., G. G. A., Greif A.; one daughter, Eliza. She married a Mr. Joe Wright; remained in Virginia up to this date, raising a large and respectable family. Her brother, Greif Adams, remained up to his death, and raised quite a large and self-sustaining family. He died about 1878.

Burwell B., the oldest son, was born October 8, 1800; remained in Virginia up to November 2, 1826, when he married a Miss Amanda M. F. Harwell, who was born in Dinwiddie county, Va., on April 25 1807. After marriage they moved immediately to McNairy county, Tenn., soon after Purdy, the county site, was established, where he lived. He was clerk in the first store, which was opened by J. T. Burtwell. Soon afterwards he was made deputy surveyor under Maj. B. Wright, and they surveyed the lands of the county, and part of North Mississippi they helped sectionize; afterwards became merchant and hotel keeper

B. B. Adams.

he then was elected entrytaker, which office he filled eight years; afterwards appointed census-taker. He was one of the first founders of Methodism in the county. His house was the home of the church and prodigal wanderer; a man beloved by all who knew him. He lived in Purdy up to the year 1857, where all his children were born, five sons and three daughters, named T. L. A., Cincinatus C. A., Herbert L. A., John R. A. and Marcus M. A.; daughters—Elizabeth V. A., Julia A. A. A., and Amanda F. A., all now living except Elizabeth V., C. C., and M. M. A. He moved to Chewalla, Tenn., in the year 1856; was depot agent and in the mercantile business for several years; then moved from there to Corinth, Miss., where he died November 26, 1871, being about 71 years old. Next, G. G. A., the second son of Jeremiah A., came out to Purdy, Tenn., in the year 1827, being married in Virginia to Miss Priscilla Combs about two years before he moved. He brought his father and mother-in-law with him, two very intelligent and pious old people, the parents of Tom, Gilbert and Jack Combs, all good citizens, who moved out soon afterwards. There were also two daughters who came out, Mrs. Parmer Pearson and Mrs. Betsey Stanley, both estimable ladies. Mrs. Stanley still living in McNairy; Mrs. Pearson dead. The old man Combs lived to the age of seventy-six and a half; old lady eighty-eight, then died. G. G. A. was a man of excellent morals and good business qualities. They lived in and around Purdy until all of their children were born—eleven in number; four died at an early age; seven were raised to womanhood and manhood, five sons and two daughters, all who grew up to be men and women of good standing. G. G. A. left Purdy in 1852; moved to Bolivar; in 1858 to Grand Junction, Tenn.; then to Iuka, Miss. All the time in good active business. He was noted for his morality. I have heard him say he never swore an oath, chewed or smoked tobacco, drank a dram, or loved but one woman. He lived at Iuka, Miss., up to his death, June 6, 1868. He was born November 26, 1801, in Bedford county, Va. After Burwell B. A. and G. G. A. moved out to Purdy, Tenn., their father, Jeremiah, followed them in about the year 1834, bringing with him four sons and one daughter, all of whom were single—J. M. A., Robert A., J. E. A., and P. P. A, sons; daughter, Susan, and he settled in about one and a half miles southwest of Purdy on a good farm, which was worked with a fine number of good and faithful negroes. He was a great sportsman, and the hills and hollows was made to echo with the sound of his horn and hounds, and his house was the great rendezvous of his many friends who participated with him in his sports and hospitality. He was a man of great piety and morality. His wife died March 31, 1849. They both lived to about the age of 73 years. They had the pleasure of seeing all of their children married. The first after they moved out was J. M. A. to Miss Ann Hamilton. They remained in the neighborhood of Purdy until their children became grown, which were seven sons and two daughters, all noted for their fine and manly appearance, and their self-sustaining qualifications. He died about the spring of 1879, his widow moving to Humboldt, Tenn., where she now lives with her son.

Susan, the daughter of Jerry A., was married to I. P. Young in the year 1836, a man of fine intellect and business qualifications. He moved from Purdy in about the year 1842 to Farmington, Miss., where he merchandised until the M. & C. Railroad was built and Corinth, Miss., was established, moving to that place as one of its first merchants. He and his wife both died there. He lived to the age of 80 years; his wife about 67. They raised five children, three daughters and two sons, all of whom were married in Corinth, Miss. They died very devoted Christians. James E. A. lived with his father up to his marriage. He was united to a Miss Arilla Dickens. He had but two children, son and daughter; moved out to Texas in about 1851. His son is an eminent doctor. J. E. A. is living now in Anderson county, Texas. Col. Robert A. served the county of McNairy as their county clerk; also a prominent merchant. Was married to Miss Sarah Young, a sister of I. P. Young, about the year 1839; had two children, son and daughter. He died in 1843. His widow and two children still live in Purdy. The daughter, Mary D., was married to Mr. John Harris, a merchant, and one of the most prominent citizens of the county. The son, John R. A., was married to Miss Mary Dilahunty. Dr. P. P. Adams moved from Purdy, Tenn., to Farmington, Miss., in 1840; made considerable distinction as a practitioner; was married in the neighborhood to a Miss Mary Chambers; they then moved out to Texas with his brother J. E. A. He there represented the people in Congress. He died in 1878, being married to his second wife, Miss Lucy Serratt, near Corinth, Miss., leaving his widow and three sons in Texas, two of them prominent lawyers, the other not grown

I will note, Adamsville, McNairy county, was named for G. G. Adams, one of her best and most thriving towns. The first rat that was ever seen in the county was in Purdy in the moving of a pole-cabin built by Maj. B. Wright, located in the northern part of the town, moved for the purpose of putting up a frame building. When the pioneer rat, dispossessed of his home and killed, their was a number of grown persons there that had never seen one before, and caused as much excitement as if a lion had been slain.

T. L. ADAMS.

JOHN G. RANDOLPH.

John G. Randolph was born in North Carolina 1795; when quite young moved to Wilson county, Tenn.; his mother died when he was quite a child; his father enlisted in the war of 1812 with his two sons, Greef and Paton; the former was captured and carried to Quebec by the British; when this intelligence reached him he immediately went to war, but was too young to carry his musket in marching or drilling; served through the war; then served five years longer as a regular; his father died and was buried during the war at Pensacola; he returned to his home in Wilson county; remained there a few years; then was married near Jackson, Tenn., to Miss N. Gayle Wynne; they remained in Wilson county till 1838, when he went to McNairy county; engaged in the agricultural pursuits: was a man of great energy and perseverance, consequently accumulated vast amounts of lands, and was an extensive slave owner; his house was the preacher's home; whenever called on for contribution to support any church or educational enterprise he responded freely and liberally; gave $100 yearly to foreign missions; gave $500 at one time to the missionary cause; was a member of the Methodist Church; politically was a Democrat; had ten children—six girls and four boys; all lived to be grown except one, who died at 7 years. Sarah married Wm. Murchison; Lizzie, Dr. J. McKinney; John, Ruth Baskwell; Sam died a prisoner in the late war at Camp Douglass; Martha, T. L. Adams; Mary died at the age of 16; Capt. G. W., Lula Moore, who died; then he mar-

Jno. G. Randolph

ried Lela Coleman; Polk, Bettie Duke (daughter of Fountain P. Duke;) Lavinia died at 7 years; Allie, Dr. Larwill. His wife died in 1878 at the age of 73; was a lady of remarkable piety. Soon after her death he left Montezuma, his old home, to spend the remainder of his days with his daughter, Mrs. T. L. Adams, in Corinth, Miss., where he lived only a few months; returned to his old home on business, and while there died. MATT. ADAMS.

CHANEY—BURTWELL.

Jacob Chaney and wife were both born in New London, Conn., about November, 1793, being about the same age.

The Burtwell family, of which Mrs. Chaney was a member, moved from New London to Ohio. The family consisted of Capt. Thomas Burtwell and his wife Col. John T. Burtwell, James, George and Mary. The elder Burtwell died in Ohio. Jacob Chaney and Mary Burtwell were married in Portsmouth, Ohio, in 1819. They removed from there to Purdy at an early date. Col. John T. Burtwell commenced the business of a merchant in Purdy, and soon afterwards married Miss Cornelia Bedford, of Florence, Ala. He subsequently moved to Florence, and died there. Mr. and Mrs. Chaney had four children—Charles, the eldest who died without marrying; Samuel, who married Miss Mary Purdy, of Henderson, county, daughter of Colonel John Purdy; Rebecca, who married Robert Purdy, brother of Samuel's wife, and Elizabeth, who first married Frank Bell, who died a few years after their marriage, and she subsequently married Mr. Whitesides.

Doctor Samuel Chaney died at Guntown, Miss., in 1875, leaving two boys, who now live in Texas. Mrs. Whitesides has a daughter by her first marriage.

Mrs. Purdy (Rebecca) resides at Henderson Station, Tenn, and has five sons and two daughters.

THE HISTORY OF THE HILL'S AND THEIR EARLY SETTLEMENTS IN McNAIRY.

There are many things to admire and imitate in the character of the Hill people. In the history of the whole generation, not one ever gazed through a prison bar or brought disgrace in any manner upon the name. They are generally happy and contented; with a determination to win. Their education, generally, is upon an average, good though it has been much neglected. Their chief occupation is farming, and not many have ever left it to follow any other. Their home is considered their place of retreat; and preferring the warmth of their firesides to the pleasures of the outside world, they are never happier than when surrounded by those whom they love. Being of English and Irish descent, they are all well developed men and women. They are noted for their longevity. Their average duration of life is 65 years. Many have lived far beyond it—not many beneath it.

They have been citizens of McNairy ever since the first settlements, they having moved to this county in the year 1828. They came from Jefferson county, East Tennessee, and settled three miles north of Purdy, on Cypress Creek. Then McNairy presented a wild and desolate appearance. Wolves howled in the wilderness; panthers screamed in the jungle; large herds of deer grazed undisturbed on the sandy hills; while smaller game, such as squirrels and rabbits, played "bast" along the mossy streams. There was nothing of a civilized nature to be seen. Purdy, itself, only contained a few huts, and a rude log court house.

There were no churches, no mills, and in fact, nothing that denoted an upward tendency; but, however, they found such land as best suited them, and, as was the custom then, they were contented, notwithstanding the deficiencies to wear patched clothes, and to hope for a better future.

The first mill that was erected in the settlement was built by Anthony Street on Cypress, on what is now known as the McCallum place. The first church and school house was built near Cypress, at what is now known as Plunk's mills, in 1830. The first school was taught by Daniel Griffin. It was composed of students from all the surrounding settlements within ten miles. Then it was not considered a hardship to go ten miles to school; but now it is rather a difficulty for the boys to go one-fourth of a mile. Some of the leading men in McNairy to-day were educated at this school. In the same year, and at the same place, a church was organized under the management of the Primitive Baptists, Franklin Beard acting as pastor. This settlement, known to-day as the Hill settlement, was among the largest then in the county. It was composed of old man Daniel Hill, Sr., and his eight sons and families, together with his sons-in-law, Isaiah Coffman, Thomas Griffin, and their families ; and old Ben Walker, William Beatty, Samuel Houston, the Wilson and Rankin families

The old generation has passed away, leaving their work in the hands of their children, which number seventy-five, now living in McNairy. Great changes have taken place since then. Instead of carrying our cotton to Memphis, as was the custom then, we find a market at home. The new age has brought many revolutions. The old one was buried in the "sweet long ago." The future opens her fields for improvement. LaFayette Hill.

WM. H. BEAVERS.

In 1835 Wm. H. Beavers removed from Giles county, Tenn., and settled at what was known as the Oxford place, seven miles south of Purdy.

He was elected a representative to the General Assembly in 1837, and during his term an act was passed chartering a turn-pike road from Purdy to Chambers, leading south a distance of fifteen miles. The act provided that the stock at the rate of fifteen thousand dollars per miles should be taken half by a stock company and the other half by the State.

On adjournment of the General Assembly Beavers returned home, and organized a company among his friends, who subscribed for half the stock, and elected directors, officers, &c.

The proper certificate was made out, signed and sent to the Governor, and he appointed an equal number of directors. They met and borrowed the money, paid up subscriptions for stock and put the whole road under contract to Beavers. They drew the State's half of the subscription out of the treasury, and repaid the men from whom they had borrowed. On a further certificate to the Governor that the individual stock had been paid up, State bonds to the amount of seventy-five hundred dollars were issued to Beavers, which he invested in Nashville in a stock of goods, and brought them to Purdy and commenced business on a large and very liberal scale. The turn-pike was never built, and Beavers, after disposing of his goods, moved to Texas.

Respectfully,
N C Riggs

The GOOCH FAMILY.

Thomas Gooch married Annie Gillentine in North Carolina. Came to Mc-Nairy county in 1827. Had four sons, viz: J. G. Gooch, Jessie Gooch, Nicholas Gooch and William Gooch, and two daughters, Margaret Gooch and Mary Gooch.

John G. Gooch married Lavina Brumlow in 1830, by whom he had nine children, three girls and six boys. In 1844 his wife died. He was married again in May, 1845, to Nancy A. Rains, by whom he had thirteen children, five boys and eight girls—in all eleven sons and eleven daughters. He was elected a justice of the peace in McNairy county in 1836, and has held that position ever since, and has been Chairman of the County Court a great number of years.

Jessie Gooch married Loucinda Rains in 1836, by whom he had six sons and six daughters.

Nicho las Goo married Marry Ann Rains in 1836, by whom he had three sons and three daughters.

William Gooch married Sarah McNalt, by whom he had four sons and four daughters.

Margaret Gooch married Ezekiel Dunaway in 1828, by whom she had two son and one daughter.

Mary Gooch married Wiley B. Terry, by whom she had one son and five daughters.

The occupation of the Gooch family in the main was farming. In religious principles they were old Primitive Baptists. Politically they were old Line Henry Clay Whigs.

The children and grand-children of the old stock, which run up into the hundreds, are mostly citizens of McNairy county at present, and have ever been peaceable law abiding citizens, and have contributed as much to the development of the resources of the county as any family in the county.

NELSON CARRINGTON RIGGS.

Nelson Carrington Riggs was born in Orange county, North Carolina, December 17, 1810. His father, John Riggs, married a Miss Carrington. John Riggs was a farmer and shoemaker. He was a man at that time like most North Carolinians who came to this county—of small means. Nelson C. was the oldest child. His parents moved to Henderson county, Tenn., when he was 10 years old. He lived with his parents, together with six brothers and sisters, in Henderson county until he was in his majority, when he moved to McNairy county, and engaged. On October 7, 1833, he married a Miss Blakely, and lived with her happily in their humble home for several years, when she died. There was born unto them Marcus L. Riggs, who reached manhood, and during the war was a Confederate soldier in the 154th Tennessee Regiment; was killed in line at Franklin, Tenn. He was at that time the only grown son of Nelson C., and was an exceedingly popular and brilliant man. His loss was keenly felt by his father. After the death of his first wife he married Emily Blackshire on March 21, 1844, with whom he lived and had born to them three children, the only one now surviving being R. B. Riggs, a young man now married and living in Purdy. His second wife died in 1853, and he married Miss Angie McLaughlin, with whom he lived in Purdy until her death, in 1876. In February, 1878, he again married, Miss Maggie L. Pharr, with whom he lived until his death, which occurred very suddenly on the morning of May 22, 1880. At the age of 30 he joined the Methodist Episcopal Church (South.) He was a devoted Christian and Sunday-school worker. Was superintendent of the Purdy Sunday-school at the time of his death. He believed in heartfelt religion, and was prominent as a public worker in all revivals. He held the office of Sheriff for many years in the county. Was Clerk and Master of the Chancery Court after the war. He was an old Line Whig, with strong feelings in his political belief. During the war he was an inactive Unionist, and after the war an independent voter. He had, by a peculiar diligence to the question of finance, accumulated quite a respectable fortune, and was actively engaged in making money at the time of his death. He had many warm friends drawn to him by his force of character, his strict sense of honor and duty, and many other noble qualities possessed by him in an eminent degree. Nelson C. Riggs was truly a self-made man, for he had few advantages in early life, but his example shows what a man can make of himself, when he determines to make the best of the advantages God has given him. He was a man of fine intellect, and rare judgment. He never did anything hastily or from impulse, but weighed every matter with careful consideration, and seldom failed to meet with success. He was a kind and considerate husband and father, and was never happier than when in the sacred precincts of his home. His loss is greatly felt by many in the county, for he was a staunch friend, and a friend in need to many. He lies in the Purdy cemetery, where a white shaft marks his last resting place, and flowers strewn by loving hands bedeck the new made grave. His memory will remain long in the hearts of many of the people of McNairy county.

J. W. P

A SKETCH OF JAMES WARREN.

BY MRS. JENNIE S. PERKINS.

Very few self-made men exist who have come up through greater difficulties than the subject of this sketch. Left an orphan, and penniless at a very early age, he with his brother John, were bound out, as was the custom of those days ; and as was too often the case to a hard, unfeeling master, whose treatment became so unbearable that the boys fled to the mountains to escape his cruelty They were not wholly forsaken, however, for sympathizing friends, who were cognizant of their whereabouts, fed the fugitives until their persecutor was induced to relinquish his claim on them. They were then bound to Henry Lebo, with whom they lived until the death of the latter, when they were transferred to Stanford Saunders, a son-in-law of Lebo. Saunders removed from East Tennessee to McNairy county, West Tennessee, bringing James and John Warren with him. John tired of his position, and left before his term of service expired ; but James faithfully served out his time, and then with the means that was due him on becoming of age, began to act on his own responsibility.

He soon after inter-married with Miss Eliza Rains, a most excellent lady, who has proved a very worthy helpmate.

He soon began holding office, rising step by step, until elected representative from his county to the Legislature.

He in the meanwhile carried on his farm, and by industry and strict attention to business steadily accumulated wealth.

He was a Whig before the war, and loyal to the Government during the

Jno. G. Gooch

strife, but never violent. In politics since the war he has opposed radicalism, being inclined to a lenient policy with those disaffected towards the United States Government.

For many years he resided near Purdy, but lately he removed several miles southwest from the county seat, where he has reared a beautiful home, and surrounded himself and family with all the solid comforts of life.

His life-long friends have recently given further testimony of their appreciation of his merits by electing him to the State Senate.

Few men have been so successful in all the relations of life; for to wealth and popularity have been added great domestic felicity, and children that are an honor to the parents who reared them.

The view of such a career gives abundant evidence that faithfulness in all the duties of one's position brings the reward promised to him, who, having been "faithful over a few things, small be made ruler over many things."

DRS. RICHARD AND CHARLES CRUMP.

BY MRS. J. S. PERKIN.

Doctors Richard and Charles Crump were resident physicians of Purdy more than forty years ago. They were highly esteemed, being graduates of the famous Medical College of Lexington, Ky.

They were both very popular, although radically different in their leading characteristics.

In personal appearance Richard was very striking, and perhaps no man in his day made more impression on the society in which he moved, o'- inspired warmer friendships, which he has warmly returned. He was impulsive, talented, and eccentric in the highest degree; vivacious, fond of dancing, singing sentimental songs, and all the innocent amusements, at the same time possessed of deep religious feeling, and strong faith in an overruling Providence, without the least admixture of Puritanism.

As an illustration of his peculiarities, I will cite an instance related by himself. He was out hunting, and his way lay through the tall grass that covered much of the country then Presently a long sharp blade of grass sawed him in the eye, hurting him severely. The sudden pain provoked an oath before he had time to think; but with reflection came repentance, and to use his own expression, he "knuckled down right there, and prayed for forgiveness;" and he further added he had no doubt but that it was granted This is but one instance of many of his child-like faith and singularity. His sincerity, singleness of heart and charity gave abundant proof of his purity of purpose.

As a physician he inclined to follow the theory of medicine, rather than study the ever-changing types of disease, and direct his practice accordingly. He especially relied upon the theories of Professor Dudley, of Lexington Medical College, who, with Prof. Gross, were leading characters there during the time of his attendance at the lectures at that place.

In politics he was a Whig, and engaged with all the ardor of his excitable being in his campaigns of his party.

He married Miss Elizabeth Steadman, of Purdy, a lady of wealth and great personal worth, who has long survived him. He removed from Purdy to a situation on the Tennessee river known as Crump's Landing, where he died of a complication of diseases, leaving to his family a comfortable home, and the priceless inheritance of an untarnished name.

Charles C. Crump, the younger brother, was possessed of a superior judgment, was very quiet, and studious in his habits, a close observer, and reliable friend, possessing the merits of the elder brother without his eccentricities.

He was of the same politics, but did not take a very active part in them, being more engrossed with his profession. In practice he preferred to watch disease as an enemy whom he might circumvent by superior tactics, and relied but little on the theories laid down in books. His watchful care was rewarded by eminent success among his patients whom he carefully nursed through all the varying perils of sickness.

He married Miss Elizabeth Wright, of Purdy, a daughter of Major Benjamin Wright, of that place. She was a lady of great elegance and refinement, who, after a few happy years, passed away, leaving her husband and children desolate.

After her death he removed to Middle Tennessee, leaving a vacancy in the ranks of his profession severely felt by those, who by his skill, had been relieved of suffering, and rescued from death.

Dr. Crump died at his residence at Spring Hill, Tenn., on August 7, 1882. He leaves three children by his first marriage—Mrs. Alexander, of Spring Hill ; Marcus V. Crump, of Brownsville, Tenn, and Richard O. Crump, of Milan, Tenn., and one daughter by his last marriage, Lula Crump.

WORTHINGTON—POOL.

Samuel L. Worthington, one of the old-time citizens of McNairy county, was born September 1, 1803, and was married to Miss Prisilla B. Tatum on February 28, 1830.

Two children, who were reared to manhood and womanhood, were born to them. Rachel J. M. Worthington, the eldest, was born November 28, 1830, and A. M. Worthington was born March, 18, 1833. A. M. Worthington is still living in Arkansas, and is by profession a dentist.

Rachel inter-married with R. W. P. Pool on January 18, 1849, and was the mother of several children, three of whom are still living in Purdy, Tenn. After several years of suffering she died on July 31, 1877.

Her husband, R. W. P. Pool, was born in Murray, Ky., on November 14, 1824, and became a citizen of McNairy county at the time of his marriage, in 1849. He engaged in several lines of business, and was so successful in his operations that at the time of his death he had accumulated a considerable property. He died on April 27, 1880.

Samuel L. Worthington was a farmer, and a very industrious, persevering man. He died December 3, 1877, and was consequently a few months past 74 years of age.

His wife, Prisilla B. Worthington, was born February 19, 1807, and died August 11, 1866, and was 59 years of age at the time of her death. S. L. and P B. Worthington may be fairly numbered as among the pioneer settlers of McNairy county, as they came to the county at a very early day, and both lived long lives in the county; and now rest side by side in the cemetery at Purdy.

WISDOM.

There were five brothers of the elder Wisdom, to-wit: Wm. S., Moore, Quin, Pub. and Washington.

Moore came up to manhood about 1833, was of fine size and well proportioned, full of life and activity. He was a civil officer of the county at one time, and in August, 1834, a man by the name of Furguson Ward, who was a citizen of Kentucky, and related to the Clayton family of this county, came to Purdy accompanied by Thomas Clayton. Ward got into a game of sleight of hand, with thimble and ball, in violation of the law. John H. Chamness, who was a citizen of Purdy, got out a warrant for Ward, and placed it in the hands of Wisdom. Ward got wind of the fact and fled. Wisdom pursued him three miles north of the town. Came up with him, where, after a desperate struggle, he overcome him, placed him on his own horse and rode behind him back to town. It was then 8 or 9 o'clock at night. Just as they alighted from the horse Ward stabbed Wisdom with a long knife in the stomach, of which he died in thirty minutes. Ward was indicted for murder, and Clayton as accessory, charged with furnishing Ward with the knife. They were kept in jail some four years. After many continuances Ward was tried and convicted. A new trial was granted, and the venue changed to Hardeman county, where he was convicted again. In the progress of the trial one of the jurors became sick, was discharged, and another juror selected. An appeal to the Supreme Court upon a writ of error resulted in his acquittal. Clayton was finally tried at Purdy, and was acquitted.

The other brothers left this county at an early day. Quinn went to Mississippi, Pub. to Jacksonport, Ark, and Wash. to Mississippi, and then to Lousiana. They are all long since dead.

Mrs. Wm. T. Anderson, of Jackson, Tenn., is the only surviving sister.

MRS. JENNIE S. PERKINS.

Mrs. Perkins is the eldest daughter of Lindsey Saunders, whose character, with that of several others, she has graphically sketched in this work.

She was born in McNairy county on April 8, 1832. In March, 1863, she was married to Mr. F. D. N. Perkins, of Hardin county. Mr. Perkins removed to Orange county, Florida, in the autumn of 1877, where he and his family now reside.

Mrs. Perkins displayed early taste for literature. When quite a young girl she wrote several poems, which were published in the Memphis *Appeal*, and highly commended. She has continued occasional contributions to the press, at such times as her domestic duties would permit, and her writings are read with great pleasure, especially in Florida. She will soon publish a book of poems.

DENNY.

Alvan Denny was born in Gilford county, N. C., February 8, 1816; moved to Tennessee in November, 1827; married Emily P. Burney in July, 1849; raised five children—four sons and one daughter, all of whom are living. He died June 25, 1875.

Emily P. Burney was born in Gilford county, N. C., February 12, 1822; moved to Tennessee in 1830; was married as above stated, and is still living near Purdy.

WILLIAM S. WISDOM.

BY MRS. JENNIE S. PERKINS.

Among the celebrities of McNairy county there is none who ranked higher as a successful man than the one whose name heads this article.

Commencing without any capital, save industry, energy, and great financial capacity, he was the architect of his own fortune, and his name became a power, not only with the moneyed men of his own section, but among the merchant princes and bankers of distant cities.

What Girard was to Philadelphia, or Vanderbilt is to New York, William S. Wisdom was to McNairy county, and "as rich as Wisdom" passed into a proverb many years before his demise.

He was a man of firm will, and strong prejudices, and like all self-made men, was impatient of contradiction, and disposed to break down all opposition ; but kind to inferiors, and a notably indulgent husband and father.

He was handsome in person, possessed great tact, and suavity of manner winning many friends among those with whom he came in contact by his charming address.

He was a staunch Whig before the war, and espoused the cause of the South when Tennessee seceded.

He was twice married—first to Miss Jane Anderson, a most excellent woman, and the mother of his children. The second time to Mrs. Celia Shull, of Purdy, a woman remarkable for her energy, and faithfulness in all the relations of life. His children have inherited many of his leading traits, and his eldest son, Colonel D. M. Wisdom, has shown remarkable talent as an editor.

W. S. Wisdom united with the Christian Church, and was baptised a few months before his death, and in its faith he passed away, leaving a memory that will not perish with this generation.

KINCAID—SAWYERS.

James Kincard and family moved to Purdy from Jackson, Tenn., at an early day. He took charge of the brick tavern on the public square, which he kept until his death. He was succeeded by his son, Andrew J. Kincaid, well-known to McNairians as "Jack Kincaid." He was a man of the most indomitable energy and pluck. He contracted for and built the larger part of the Mobile and Ohio Railroad through the county. He was a prosperous merchant for many years. He moved from Purdy to Corinth a few years ago, where he died. James Bryant, a grandson of the elder Kincaid, came with him to Purdy, and died while quite young. A widowed daughter with two sons, Calyer F. and Reese P. Sawyers, were also of the family. The widow subsequently married Varnum Ozment, and died. Calyer, the eldest son, lived (for many years and up to a late date, when he moved to Palestine, Tex.,) in Corinth, Miss.

Reese P., the second son, married Miss Knox, of Hardin county. He was a banker in Mobile for several years, and resided some years at Corinth, Miss. He now resides in New Jersey, having a business office in New York city. He is a man very much like his Uncle "Jack Kincaid," of great energy and pluck, and has several times amassed comfortable fortunes, which he has lost by reverses, but his motto is *nil desterandum*, and he knows "no such word as fail."

COL. DEW. M. WISDOM,

the eldest son of the late Wm. S. Wisdom, was born at Medon, Madison county, Tenn., February 3, 1836. He is a man of marked character and acknowledged ability. He distinguished himself as a Confederate officer in the late war, and won rapid and deserved promotion. He once resided in North Mississippi, and was a member of the Legislature of that State. He held for many years the responsible office of Chancery Clerk at Jackson, where he has resided for a number of years up to a recent date, when he moved to Fort Smith, Ark. e is an accomplished scholar, a ready and graceful writer, and a man who never fails to make friends. He married Miss Annie Terry, the daughter of his father's old friend and partner in business.

Peter, the second son, now dead, married a daughter of the late M. A. Trice. John L., the youngest son, married Miss Kate Meriwether, of Jackson, Tenn., where he now resides. Maria, the eldest daughter, married A. J. Kincaid, deceased. She resides at Corinth, Miss. Mary D. married Calvin Shull, and resides in Jackson, Tenn. Sue married John H. Duke, and resides in Jackson. Hettie married P. H. Tapp, and resides in Louisville, Ky. Loraine married J H. Allen and resides in New Orleans

LORANCE.

Abram Lorance came from Chatham county, North Carolina, to McNairy county, Tenn., in the year 1824, and located in the north part of the county, where he lived to the age of, perhaps, 90 to 100 years.

His children were Elizabeth, who married John Plunk ; raised a large family, and she is now living in the country in her 87th year of her age. Jacob Lorance, who married Susan Gage, who was a daughter of Aaron Gage, who came to the county about the same time, and who had been a soldier in the Revolutionary war, and raised a small family, but one of whom are now living in the county. Jacob Lorance was an excellent good citizen and farmer, and held the office of justice of the peace and county trustee for many years, and died recently in the 79th year of his age.

Isaac, a younger brother, left the county at an early day, and his whereabouts are not known.

Some Plunk families came to the county about the same time. They were of German descent. They multiplited rapidly, and many of their descendents are now citizens of the county, and are generally industrious farmers. J. W.

JOHN BELL.

John Bell was one of the early settlers. He married a Wilson. He died many years ago He had two sons—Robert and Frank. The latter married Elizabeth Chaney, and he has been dead several years. His daughter married Isaac W. Nash, and now resides in Purdy.

JEREMIAH CLOUD.

Jeremiah Cloud was perhaps the largest man physically who ever lived in McNairy. His weight at one time reached over four hundred pounds. He died many years since.

T. F. ANDERSON

was born in Caldwell county, Ky., October 29, 1805.   His grandfather, Thos. A., was banished from Scotland to Ireland on account of his religion: left Ireland on account of the Catholic rebellion, and came to the United States; settled in North Carolina; was a soldier of the Revolution under General Green, and participated in the battle of Gilford, N. C.   James Anderson, father of T. F. A., was born February 17, 1777, in Gilford, N. C.   His father, Thomas, moved from North Carolina to Tennessee, and settled at Nashville when James was 13 years old. Moved from there to Logan county, Ky., two years afterwards to escape from the hostile Indians.   Then in Logan county, Thomas A., grandfather of T. F. A., died. James A., father of T. F. A., married August 20, 1801, to Margaret Gilmore. Her father, also a soldier in the Revolutionary war, was wounded in the battle of Savannah.   James A., father of T. F., moved from Kentucky to Tennessee in 1812.   Settled in Lincoln county.   Moved from there to Limestone, Ala., in 1820, and to Hardeman county, Tenn., in 1827.   T. F. Anderson was married in Hardeman county, Tenn., in 1834, to Jane Gates in the immediate neighborhood, where Hickory Valley now stands.   Moved from there to Tippah county, Miss., in 1836.   From there to McNairy county, Tenn., in 1844.   The family are Presbyterians.

In politics they are Democrats, and have been ever since the day of Thomas Jefferson.

T. F. A. has been a citizen of McNairy county since 1844, and has served twice as justice of the peace.   Raised a family of six children, four of whom are yet living.

His oldest son, Wm. P. Anderson, married Matilda C. Gill, moved to Arkansas in 1860; soon volunteered in the Confederate service in a cavalry regiment; soon after died at a hospital in Little Rock, Ark., of congestion of the brain.

R. D. Anderson, his second son, married Eliza A. Kerr soon after the close of the late war; is living now in the Sixth Civil District of McNairy county, Tenn., engaged in agriculture.

His third son, R. V. A., died July 29, 1861, of typhoid fever at the age of 19.

His fourth son, J. G. A., married Emma Basinger, and is a citizen of Mc-Nairy county.

His oldest daughter, Susan C. A., is not married, is the only child remaining under the parental roof.

Martha J. Anderson married James McKinzie, and is now living in Wise county, Texas.

NEWSPAPERS.

It is in the recollection of the writer that the first newspaper published in McNairy county was by Isaac W. Nash, and called the *West Tennessee Argus*.   It was started in 1857.

There are two papers now in Purdy, the *Sun*, and the *Independent*, the former, a Democratic paper, edited by Dr. Daniel Barry, the latter by J. W. Purviance Purviance which is Independent in politics.

The *Independent* was first issued March 15, 1879, and has never missed a publication, and its columns have been largely devoted to the material interests of the county.   Both papers are well patronized.

ADAM WEAVER

was born in the State of North Carolina in 1769. Came to Wilson county, Tenn., date not remembered. Raised a family of twelve children:

Sons—

Absalom	married	Elizabeth Rupard.
John	"	Mary McMillan.
Joshua	"	Miss Taylor.
Lewis	"	Miss Nelson.

Daughters—

Elizabeth	married	John Lynch.
Dedemiah	"	Jacob Crouse.
Nancy	"	John Morris.
Fanny		died.
Teny	"	William Russel.
Two others		died.

John Weaver came to McNairy county in 1825. Located in the northwestern part of the county when a wilderness. He had been a soldier in the war of 1812-15. He raised a family of nine children.

Isaac	married	Susan Muse.
William	"	Sarah Pope.
John	"	Carodis Pope.
George	"	Susan Yates.
Daniel	"	Lavina Ward.
Robert	"	Mary Highfield.
James	"	Susan James.
Mathew		died.
Mary	"	Joel Pope.

William Weaver, who furnished this sketch, is living at Montezuma, now Chester county, and has two children.

Mary Ann	married	W. T. Muse.
Margaret	"	William Lane.

The Weavers were in the main farmers, and many of them are living in the county.   J. W.

JOHN S. JOPLING

John S. Jopling was born in Nelson county, Va., in the year 1781. His father, who was a native of Scotland, moved to Buckingham county, Va., soon after, where John S. grew up to manhood, and married a Miss Jane Laird, who was a native of Ireland, in the year 1820. In 1836 he came to McNairy county, and located three miles south of Purdy, where he raised a family of seven children. William, who married Araminta Dickins, who, after bearing two children, died. His second wife was Julia Walsh.

Maria married W. P. Basinger; Andrew died soon after manhood; Sarah died in early womanhood; James F. married Silvia S. Luttrell; Rebecca married William H. Baker; Benjamin S. married Margaret Olivar.

John S. Jopling was a farmer with reasonable success. Raised their family in good credit and respectability. Died in 1869, in the 87th year of his age. His wife, who was ten years younger, died in 1870, lamented by all who knew them.

JAMES BROOKS

was born in Chatham county, North Carolina, in the year 1788. Came to Tennessee in the year 1805. Located in Maury county. On arriving at manhood he married Miss Esther Hopkins.

They had four children—Aaron Mose and Samuel, and one daughter, Emaline. His wife died in the year 1819. He afterward married a widow lady, Mrs. Jane Beaty, by whom he had four sons—Hezekiah, Robert, Isaac and Franklin. He came to McNairy county in the year 1834, and located one and a half miles south of Purdy, where he raised his family, and they married as follows:

Aaron to Miss Ann Harris; Moses to Miss Ussery; Samuel to Mrs. Mary Miller; second wife, Nancy Young; Emaline to Mr. Thomas Luther; Hezekiah in Mississippi; name not known, and now living in Corinth, Miss.; Robert to Katharine Moore; Isaac to a Miss Hurst. Louisa, the eldest daughters of Mrs. Beaty, married Alfred Moore, for many years a merchant in Purdy.

James Brooks died in 1854; he was a good farmer; raised his family in good credit and respectability. The most of his descendants are now living in the county.

COX.

Javan Cox was born in North Carolina. When he was about 16 years old he was drafted and put in the army of the Revolution. When he was mustered in there were five brothers of them in the American army at the same time, and all went through and got home safely. He married Ede Miller, by whom he had twelve children, but only raised four—three daughters and one son, and but two of them had any family. Wm. Cox raised a large family; moved with them to Texas in 1859, and died there. Elizabeth Cox, daughter of Javan Cox, was born in Currituck county, North Carolina, June 23, 1791, and was married to George Etheridge in 1812. There were no children by this marriage. Captain Cox, with all his family, moved to Kentucky. Capt. Cox moved thence to Mississippi, and from thence to McNairy county, Tenn., in the year 1826, where his wife died in 1833. Capt. Cox was married twice after that, but there were no children from either marriage. He died in 1858, being some where near 90 years old.

CHAPTER X.

The Maxedon, Cason, Hooker, Jones, Keter, Brown, Warren, Tatum, Beck, Meeks, Devault, Kendal, Barry, and Browder Families—The County Court the first Monday in August, 1842—Peter Gullett—David Holt—School Teachers—Col. D. A. Street—Hatter Adams—Dr. McKissick—L. D. McKissick—Wm. D. Jopling—Mrs. Jennie S. Perkins.

MAXEDON.

John Maxedon was born in Scotland. Came to America, and settled in South Carolina, where he raised several children—all girls. Thomas Maxedon married Elizabeth Woody, on Haugh river, North Carolina, by whom he had eight children—five boys and three girls. William Maxedon was the oldest. He was born in South Carolina, Union District, November 16, 1791. William Maxedon's father moved to the present State of Indiana Wm Maxedon, at the breaking out of the war of 1812, volunteered in Captain Robbs' company, and was in the war till it closed. He married the widow Ethridge, who was formerly Elizabeth Cox, and daughter of Javan Cox. They moved to McNairy county, Tenn., in 1826 to the north part of the county, where they made two crops, and then moved in February, 1829, to the center part of the county, seven miles west of Purdy, near Bethel Springs.

W. H. D. Maxedon married Mary Ann Cheshier on August 21, 1845. She was a native of North Carolina; born in Roan county, but raised in Hardeman county, Tenn. From this union there were fourteen children born, thirteen of whom are now living, the oldest 36, and the youngest 8 years old; eight married and living in this county; both still living, and have thirty grandchildren.

Ede Elizabeth Maxedon was first married to Daniel Lock, by whom she had seven children, but only raised three of them to be grown, all of whom are living in this county. Lock died, and she married John Warren.

JOSEPH CASON,

a native of South Carolina, married Miss Rebecca Miller in 1776. Came to Tennessee in 1805. Located in Wilson county. He raised a family of ten children—five sons and five daughters, who married as follows:

James	married	Miss Jane McKnight.
Jeremiah	"	" Elizabeth Favor.
William	"	" Mary McKnight.
John	"	" Elvirie Miles.
Joseph	"	" Jerman.
Margaret	"	Mr. Julius Williams.
Sarah	"	" Fountain Robertson
Elizabeth	"	" Samuel Bell.
Lockey	"	Dr. Jackson.
Rebecca	"	Mr. William Winston.

William, the third son, came to McNairy county in 1826. Located in a good country in the northwest corner of the county. He opened a farm that was fertile, and although his means were small, by industry and frugality, he ac. cumulated property rapidly. He raised a family of five children, as follows:

C. M. Cason ....married Mary Barham.
Joseph Cason..................................... " Margaret Dixon.
William Cason..................................... " Jane Hamilton.
T. K. Cason..................................... died.
Rhoda Ann Cason..................................... " F. M. Ballard.

They were educated the very best the country schools afforded, and all well qualified for business. They were members of the Methodist Church, and up to the war of 1861 had accumulated a handsome fortune. Wm. Cason was once a constable, and also held the office of deputy sheriff for six years under Warren. He and his wife at this date are living at Henderson, the county seat of Chester county. He is in the 78th year of his age and his wife in the 80th year of her age.

SAMUEL B. HOOKER

was born in North Carolina in 1779. Came to East Tennessee at an early day of its settlement. Married Miss Barsheba Noland Came to McNairy in 1829. Located in the Ninth Civil District, southeast part of the county. Raised a family of nine children.

William M...................................married Eliza Patterson.
Elizabeth..................................... " John Wardlow.
A. J...................................... " Nancy Hooker, 2d cousin
Ann.. " Gilbert Woodard.
H. H....................................... " Jennie Caruthers.
Susan J..................................... " William Hooker.
Thomas B.................................... " Miss Baker.
John....................................... " Nancy Clear.
Sirena..................................... " Monroe Ozburn.

Samuel B. Hooker was a farmer. Raised his family to industry. Gave them a common school education. Many of his descendants have gone West; some remaining in the county. He lived to a ripe old age, and died in the county in the 87th year of his age.

JACOB JONES

was an early settler in the northern part of the county, and a man of high character for probity and intelligence.

His eldest daughter married Julius Jones, now a resident of Jackson, Tenn.

HARTWELL KETER AND ICHABOD BROWN

settled early in the northern part of the county. They came from North Carolina, and were a *mongrel* creed of people. They were quiet, honest farmers, who had the respect of their neighbors.

DR. SMITH

settled at an early day near W. T. Anderson in the northern part of the county. He had several sons and two daughters. The eldest daughter, Mary, resides now Jackson, Tenn., having twice married. The second daughter, Sallie, married _____ Robbins. She is now a widow residing in Henderson county.

Wm Cason

HON. STANFORD L. WARREN

the eldest son of Hon. James Warren, is a native of McNairy county. He was a schoolmate of the writer, and at an early day evinced uncommon talent. He was a decided Union man, and enlisted in the 6th Tennessee Union Cavalry in September, 1862. He was appointed 2d lieutenant and adjutant of his regiment on September 22, 1862. He held this position until October, 1863, when he was made a captain; on March 28, 1864, he was made a major of the regiment, and was honorably mustered out of service under orders from the War Department.

He was elected Representative to the General Assembly of Tennessee for the term of 1865-66, and was afterwards appointed by President Andrew Johnson United States District Attorney for West Tennessee.

He was then again elected to the lower house of the General Assembly of Tennessee for 1869-70.

In 1871-72 he was elected to the State Senate from the district composed of the counties of Hardeman and McNairy. In 1873-74 he was again elected to the State Senate from the district composed of the counties of McNairy, Hardin, Perry, Decatur, Henderson and Benton.

Major Warren is now devoting his time to his farm and practicing his profession at Purdy. He is a man of marked ability whom the people can always rely upon as honest and upright.

Major Warren married Miss Alice L. Pharr. The names of the other children of the family are:

H. A. Warren.................................married Julia Knight.
J. T. "   .... "   Jennie Rodgers.
Nancy "   .... "   Mr. W. A. Gooch.
L. K. "   .... "   " L. H. C. Prather.
Martha "   .... "   " J. T. Jeans—

all of whom reside in McNairy county, except Jeans and wife, who are now citizens of Wooster, Ark. The oldest daughter of the family, Mary A. Warren, died at the age of 12 years. The youngest son, James F. Warren, died at the age of 9 years.

TATUM.

Edward Tatum was born in Brunswick county, Va. He moved from there to North Carolina, and was a member of the General Assembly of that State. He settled in McNairy county, Tenn., in 1830. His family consisted of seven sons and one daughter. He died at the age of 78 years, his wife having died before him. He married a second time, but there were no children by the second wife.

Of the sons, Sion resides in McNairy county; Henry moved to Texas many years since, and died; Harbert and Edward reside in Texas; the oldest son in South Carolina, and Edwin in Hardeman county, Tenn. The family always maintained a high standing.

THOMAS R. BECK

was an early settler in the southern part of the county. He is still living near Stantonville. He was for many years Clerk of the Chancery Court, and has always been a citizen of mark and influence.

JOHN MEEKS, Sr.

BY MRS. JENNIE S. PERKINS.

Although the subject of this sketch was not one of the earliest settlers of McNairy county, he spent, perhaps, forty years of his life there, and his descendants are among the most prominent of its citizens, while his unimpeachable integrity, and great purity of life are worthy of the emulation of all, and should be held in a lasting remembrance as a realization of the fact that "the memory of the just is blessed."

John Meeks, Sr., was born in the State of Virginia over one hundred years ago, and was the son of Jesse Meeks, who was a Methodist minister and a missionary among the Indians.

When young John went to Tennessee. He there married a Miss Henderson, who became the mother of General John H. Meeks, so long a prominent citizen of McNairy county. He lost his first wife soon after the birth of this son, and married a lady of superior personal and mental attractions, who became the mother of three sons and three daughters, all of whom were more than ordinarily gifted.

Orville, the eldest, represented his county in the State Legislature before the war, and filled other positions of trust, and possessed great energy and force of character. Edwin was a popular minister of the gospel. Wiles, the youngest, early displayed great financial talent. The daughters were Mrs. Mary Tuley, Mrs. Adaline Donnell, and Mrs. Martha Gibson, all of whom were favorably known in their section.

The father, although gifted with excellent common sense, was one of those rare personages whose virtues overshadow every other mental attribute.

He was more than ordinarily happy in his family relations, living to see his children's children occupying honorable positions among their fellows.

He lived to an extraordinary age, possessing his faculties in an uncommon degree to the last.

When at last more than 90 years had passed since he came upon the stage of existence he passed away, regretted and beloved by all who knew him.

JOHN DEVAULT

was born March 13, 1801. Married Frances Priddy September 12, 1823, who was born May 10, 1799.

John Devault was an early settler, and built the first jail in the county.

They had eight children, four of whom reside in the county. They have resided in the county for 55 years. They are both living with their son, Thomas Devault, three miles east of Purdy.

DR. WM. C. KENDAL,

who married the eldest daughter of Judge Valentine D. Barry, was one of the most distinguished and successful physicians of the county. He and his wife are both dead. They left a number of children.

Dr. Daniel Barry has lived in the county for many years. He is a practicing physician, and the editor of the county Democratic paper. Mrs. Eudova Miller, his sister, also resides in Purdy.

RICHARD BROWDER

settled at an early date on Oxford Creek, where he now lives at an advanced age He has always been a good citizen, and highly respected by all his neighbors.

COUNTY COURT FIRST MONDAY IN AUGUST, 1842.

BY MRS. JENNIE S. PERKINS.

We will premise that it is the first Monday in August, 1842, and that the yeomanry of McNairy county are gathering from all quarters to Purdy, the common center. Each district sends its quota, the majority on horseback, some on foot, and a very few in carriages. From the Fifth come those live men, the Chambers, busy with financial schemes—"For money had stuck to the race through life," and they are wholly occupied with the present, the great future being a blank in their creed. With them are their friends and allies, Elbert Stinson, Henry Sharp—Barnhill, Robert Houston, Sr.—like the Chambers, good citizens, who are building up their fortunes with their own section. From the Ninth Benjamin Saunders, Esq., a man of inflexible integrity, and very popular in his neighborhood. Then come Damron, Atkins, and Stubblefield, John A. Sharp and Wardlow. The citizens—Burkes, Miller, Smith Conn, Farris, Miller, George, and the Donnells. From the Tenth district Sanders McKinzy, tall, erect, and taciturn as an Indian. John Kendrick, an old Virginian, a mighty hunter, and the first Thompsonian physician in McNairy; Wm. Caruthers, whose face, hard as his own Calvinistic doctrine, seemed to say in every line, "What is to be, will be;" Old Nattie Erwin, a Presbyterian elder of high standing, liké Peter, ready to smite with the sword if necessary; Holman Duncan, the Baron Munchausen of his section; Pope Norval, the neighborhood bully; Thomas Veal, a worthy farmer; Soloman Awalt, a Presbyterian preacher; Squire Wilburn, a wealthy farmer; the saintly fathers, McCann and Rainey; Ussery, the Cardwells, the Jacksons, John Preston, Myrick, Andrew McKinzy, Ben. Howell, David McKinzy, just entering public life, and a very popular man; Reuben McKenzy, George House, "Old Puppy" Smith; Theopholus Hamm, the hunch-backed constable of the Tenth, on the *qui vive* for business; James Ellis, Thomas Tinsley, William Strawn, Tankersly, Wm. Smith, Larkin Rushing, whose high falsetto could be heard above the hum of manly voices; old man Leighton, on foot, and too indolent to speak plainly; Levi Anderson, John Gilchrist, Henry Arnhart, an old Dutchman; Wm. Shelby, Wm. Wyatt, self nick-named "Tiwopeta;" Thomas Saunders, Sr., happy in the success of his sons, (Thomas Saunders, Jr., Joel K. Saunders,) jogging quietly along, discoursing of ancient history; Lindsey Saunders, grave, dignified, and engrossed with his official duties; Benjamin Saunders, Esq., of the Tenth district, haughty, erudite, and exclusive; John Cobb, Thomas Beck, a young and aspiring man; John Green, Sprinkles, Jones, McWhirter, and Forbes.

From the Adamsville district, George Adams, the builder of the first turnpike in the county, and for whom the village was named; Jack Lindsey, Bolton, Skillman, old Jimmy Wilson, John Helbert, Joel Stanley, Anderson Cox, the Scotts, Suratts, Parmer Pierson, the Combs', old Billy Rogers, the champion distiller of McNairy county; the Carrolls, Hills, Tidwells, Higgins, Carr, Robertson, and Williams.

The crowd increases, and we lose sight of districts, but the faces and names are familiar.

There is John Paschal, Sr., the Chamnesses, the Chandlers, Birchetts, Dancers, Petersons, and the two Barneses, with the same Christian names of Charles, but distinguished by the cognomen of "Baconhead," and "Frogeye;" Pugh Cannon, with a cancer on his lip, a wooden leg, and a revolutionary pension; the Inmans,

Phillipses, Rileys, Shultzses, Baizes, K. Julian, the Rosses, Bat. Brantley, Joe Kemp, Pascal Morton, the Dineses, noted gamblers ; Jacob Blackshear, a Methodist minister; Nelson Riggs, William Hughes, Simon Landreth, hiding under a quiet exterior eminent classical attainments ; Birkeen, Butler, and Bassinger.

Northward came the noted citizens, John S. Ingraham, James Anderson, Joseph Anderson, the Smiths, Matt. Trice, in his prime, and rapidly acquiring riches and popularity ; then came Sewells, Hardins, Swains, Simpson Massengill, the O'Neils, the renowned " Hardshell " Baptist preacher; Frank Beard ; Elijah Hill, Major Horton, a rising man ; the Hightowers, Doolins, Larues, Smallwoods, and Jacob Lowrance.

From the west, the Hon. John M. Johnson, and the worthy gentlemen, Samuel Magee, Major Randolph, Fountain Duke, and Squire Gooch; Lany Moore, then a man of note; John Bell, Sr., county surveyor; the Streets, Wilsons, Rankins, Kirbys, Gillespies, Tatums, Kernodles, Youngs, and the fat man, " Old Jerry " Cloud.

From the southwest are several representatives, each from the Simpsons, Gages, Grahams, Sweats, Murrays, Styles, and McCullers.

Nearer are the Bakers, John H. Meeks, in the beginning of a prosperous career, and full of diplomacy; Lewis Carter, Sr., a thrifty farmer, as unrelenting as fate; John S. Jopling, one of the first Virginia families, a man whose creed seemed to be that "Silence is golden;" John Brooks, stern, rigidly honest, and of few words; James Warren, in the first dawn of public life.

From the Thirteenth, Stanford-Saunders, a prominent citizen of his section, intensely devoted to his political party, and whole-souled in all that he undertook ; Alfred Needham, an industrious farmer of the old school, and a first-class citizen, but angered beyond control at the assertion that the world moved ; Felix Todd, a dwarf of singular appearance, and great cunning; David Horn, Esq., the Eliss; Autens, Smiths, Magees, McCanns, Robert Rains, Esq., Robert Luttrell, Sr., Grandma Rains, with her wagon of apples, ginger bread and cider, well patronized by the hungry and thirsty crowd.

In the neighborhood of town, old Mr. Terry, Dickens, McCraw, Ray, Lumpkin, Homes, Reynolds, old Capt. Adams and his sons, Mitchell Adams and James Adams.

In Purdy, Major Wright, tately, and elegant as some knight of olden time, the French-Canadian inn-keeper, C. H. Dorion; Wyley B. Terry and Wm. S. Wisdom, merchants, just laying the foundations of a princely fortune for each ; Samuel Pace, tailor; Maclin Cross, lawyer ; the physicians, Richard Crump, Chas. Crump and Rufus Harwell; A. A. Saunders, and Richard Harwell, merchants ; Jack Kincaid, hotel keeper; Burrell Adams, Wilkerson, Jacob Chaney, the finest penman of his time; Simonton, a cabinet workman; Beavers, Malugen, the jailor ; Ruleman & Weedon, tanners ; George Burtwell and James Burtwell, owners of the carding factory ; Laird, Robert Adams, James Connor, the teacher of the Boy's Academy ; " Old Jimmy " Reed, who built all of the first brick structures in the county ; Sawyer, an *attache* of Kincaid's tavern ; Nat. Shull and " Long Tom " Johnson ; Harbert Tatum, Wisdom's clerk ; Andy McKee, W. C. Saunders, then a young man on the alert for merriments; William Jopling, boiling with energy that had not been systemized; Sam Chaney John V. Wright, Marcus J. Wright and Calvin Shull, still school boys.

What swarms of people; what a buzz of conversation as groups of men gather at the corners and discuss the leading topics of the day.

W D Jopling

The Court assembles, and the dignitaries of the common law sit in council, while the chairman presides with all gravity of a Beaconsfield or Gladstone. These squires are Nature's noblemen, who, like Cincinatus, have left their ploughs to attend the calls of duty. They possess the elements of true greatness, incorruptible integrity, and a great reverence for law and order, and the interests of their fellow-citizens are safe in their hands. They are representative men, and reflect great credit on the pioneers of McNairy county.

The idle crowd lounge in to watch the proceedings, or go to the whiskey shops to get a drink. There is much senseless bluster, rude jokes from the vulgar, dogmatic assertions from the ignorant, profanity from the drunken, and an incipient fight with the usual crowd of spectators. A few retire to Monsieur Dorion's hotel, where the affable host spreads the best of dinners at twenty-five cents *per capita*, or the brick tavern presided over by Jack Kincaid, whose fare is surpassed by none, and equalled by few, while a large number still refresh themselves with ginger cake and cider furnished by Dames, Maxwell, Rains, and Magee.

At length the momentous questions are decided, and the Court retires, the business of the day is over, and the receding tide of humanity rolls backward over the roads that beheld their ingress in the morning, and night and silence closes over the first Monday in August, 1842.

COL. DAVID A. STREET,

of Lunenburg county, Virginia, who first settled in Jackson, Tenn., after leaving Virginia, was the first classical teacher at Purdy. He was a fine scholar, wholly given up to books and teaching. He was very fond of his scholars, and entertained them at his house in the most hospitable manner. He died in Savannah, Tenn., to which place he removed with all of his children—two boys—Thomas and D. T., and two girls. His eldest son now resides in Savannah.

WM. D. JOPLING,

whose name appears elsewhere, came to the county from Virginia with his father, John S. Jopling, in 1836. He held the office of sheriff of the county in 1856-62, in 1870-76, and is the present (1882) sheriff of the county. He represented the county in the lower house of the General Assembly in 1861-63. He is a man of great and deserved popularity, and one of the best officers the county ever had.

SCHOOL TEACHERS.

To the names of early school teachers, mentioned on page 10, should be added F. M. Prince, who taught in Purdy in 1825; Wilson McMahan, in 1827; Mrs. M. B. Chaney, in 1828, and for several years afterwards; Miss Delia Swann, in 1844; Miss Loraine Hall, in 1848; Miss Maria Bomar, in 1850; Miss Rachel D. Halpin, in 1851; Miss Hattie Barbee, in 1854, and Mrs. Eudora Miller.

DAVID HOLT

settled on Sugar Creek in 1837. The Rev. Joseph Holt, a minister of the Baptist Church, son of David, now resides at Milan, Tenn. John M. Holt and N. A. Holt, the other sons, reside in Gibson county, and Susan Holt, who married —— McCaslin, resides in Carroll county.

MRS. JENNIE S. PERKINS.

A short sketch of Mrs. Perkins was given on a former page. Her valuable contributions to this work, and the reputation she has made in the literary world entitle her to a more extended notice, which has been furnished by a friend who is familiar with her history:

The subject of this sketch was the eldest child of Lindsey Saunders, Sr., a prominent citizen, and widely known and respected in his section.

She was born in McNairy county April 8, 1832. At the early age of three years she learned to read, and soon showed a decided taste for literature, devouring every book that came within her reach, especially poetical works.

She began writing verses at the age of twelve years, which were reviewed and corrected by her mother, who had a very correct idea of versification, and possessed rare intellectual gifts.

Although employing her leisure hours with composing verses, the larger portion of her time, not devoted to domestic duties, was spent in doing office work for her father, who was Circuit Clerk of McNairy county for many years. In this arduous task she was often employed all day and far into the night.

The want of encouragement, outside of the family circle, long kept her in the background, and cast a shade of melancholy over one whose inmost soul thrilled to the harmonies of song, and who longed "For something better than she had known."

Time passed on bringing its changes; but still the spirit of poetry would not be hushed, for while her hands were busy with their tasks, she sang her songs untill they were fixed in her mind, wrote them down while others slept, and laid them away for future reference.

In the summer of 1858 one was sent to her county paper, and published without comment. One or two others shared the same fate. Finally, a short poem entitled the "Stars" attracted the attention of Marcus J. Wright, a native of McNairy county, but at that time a resident of Memphis, Tenn., who, feeling an interest in his native section, wrote a letter of enquiry in regard to its authorship, and interested himself at once in the welfare of the author, giving her the encouragement and advice so greatly needed, and that so few were competent to bestow. Furthermore, in the selection and bestowal of various works of prose and poetry calculated to develop the latent talent she had evinced, and urging her to strive diligently to improve her gift.

Being a contributor himself, and otherwise connected with the Memphis *Appeal*, he advised her to contribute to the columns of that excellent paper, which she did, and received kindly encouragement, he also procured her a place among the list of contributors to the *Aurora*, an admirable magazine published also at Memphis.

To her this was the beginning of steady literary work, that was continued from early in 1859 until the breaking out of the late civil war put an end to it, and darkened the prospect that had seemed so bright. This was very discouraging, but she did not cease to write, but improved every opportunity that presented itself.

She was married on March 31, 1863, to E. D. M. Perkins, of Hardin county, Tenn., and after the close of hostilities settled in the Thirteenth Civil District of her native county, writing occasional poems, several of which were published by various papers North and South. Broken health, the result of the troubles of

Jennie S. Perkins

the late civil war, decided her husband to remove her to Florida, hoping she would receive permanent benefit from the change, and they started in the autumn of 1877, and journeyed by easy stages through the States of Mississippi, Alabama, Georgia, and far into Florida, stopping in the great orange belt of that State. The journey was replete with interest, and the weird beauty of the South has afforded much material for her fancy to appropriate. The society of her new home is of the highest order, celebrities from all quarters of the civilized world having gathered there for health or pleasure, and she has met with the most kindly recognition from its literati.

This being so she has prosecuted her literary labors with renewed vigor, and has added a great deal to the material, which she designs to embody in a book in the near future as the result of her efforts.

The people of her native section will certainly feel a pride in the fact that one of the daughters of an old pioneer has risen above the force of untoward circumstances, and been exalted to the rank of a poet.

DR. McKISSICK

was an early settler near Montezuma, in the northern part of the county. He was a very learned man, and fine physician. His eldest son, Colonel Lewis D. McKissick, has been for a number of years a distinguished lawyer in Memphis, Tenn., put is now a citizen of San Jose, Cal.

HATTER (?) ADAMS.

At an early day a hatter opened a shop in Purdy named Adams. This name being a common one, he was dubbed Hatter Adams, and his real name has passed out of the memory of the writer. He made money at his trade, and engaged in merchandise. What became of him eventually is not remembered.

PETER GULLETT

was an early settler in the county. He was connected with the old Nashville & Memphis Stage Line for many years, and eventually became a clock peddler. He had two sons and one daughter. The family moved to Humboldt some ten years ago.

BENJAMIN SELLS

was an early settler. He left the county many years since, and no data of his family has been furnished.

CONCLUSION.

The critical reader will no doubt find fault with the absence of systematic arrangement in this work. This has occurred necessarily from the manner of its publication. It is, as will be seen, mostly a compilation of sketches written by different persons, and the author and compiler desired these, as far as possible, to be printed as they were written. The articles were handed to the publisher in the order in which they were received, and hence no very systematic arrangement was possible. Should another edition be demanded more system will be observed, and it is hoped all errors will be corrected and all omissions as far as possible, will be supplied.

INDEX OF NAMES.

www.ingramcontent.com/pod-product-compliance
Lightning Source LLC
Chambersburg PA
CBHW031129020426
42333CB00012B/299